Cow in the Clinic

and Other Missionary Stories from Around the World

Introduction by
Charles D. Kirkpatrick

Light and Life Press
Winona Lake, Indiana 46590

Copyright © 1977 by
Light and Life Press

All chapters originally appeared in the *Missionary Tidings,* official publication of the General Woman's Missionary Society of the Free Methodist Church, Winona Lake, Indiana.

ISBN 0-89367-016-2

Printed in the United States of America by
Light and Life Press
Winona Lake, Indiana
46590

TABLE OF CONTENTS

Preface .... G. Roger Schoenhals   7
Introduction .... Charles D. Kirkpatrick 9

Brazil
   Missionary Without Furlough Beth Smith   13
   God Spoke to Them in a Dream Lucile Damon Ryckman   15

Burundi
   Cow in the Clinic .... Doris Moore   19

China
   Sudden Death — Sudden Glory Mary O. Schlosser   23
   The Lord's Messenger .... James H. Taylor   24
   The Power of a Bible .... Alice Hayes Taylor   26
   The Providential Gift .... E. P. Ashcraft   29
   They Called — God Answered   Alice Hayes Taylor   32
   Family Reunion .... Alice Hayes Taylor   35

Dominican Republic
   A Dominican Pastor .... Rachel M. Smiley   39

Egypt
   Undefeatable Faith .... Norman E. Cooke   42

Hong Kong
   Service from a Wheelchair .... Alton A. Gould   49
   A Miracle Overcoat .... Alton A. Gould   51

India
His Name Is Joseph	Gertrude Alcorn	53
Two Annas and a Prayer	Lois E. Kent	55
You'll Never Get Water There	Rolland N. Davis	58
Love Overcomes	Frank and Betty Kline	60
... for the Hungry	Nellie M. Jones	62

Japan
Rev. T. Kawabe's Birthday	Ruth Mylander	65
Streptomycin Have I None	Edward C. John	68
Farmer Missionaries	Alice Fensome	70

Mexico
An Evening's Report from Mexico	B. H. Pearson	74
Victor	Burleigh Willard	79

Mozambique
Moonshine in Africa	Victor W. Macy	82
Bioso	Lela DeMille	86
Down to the Sea in Ships	Mae P. Armstrong	88
Their Name Was Legion	Susan Blair Macy	90
We Have Waited a Long Time	Florence Carter	95

Paraguay
Donya Leona	Lucy Huston	99
Thanksgiving	Minoru Tsukamoto	101

Philippines
Love Conquers Fierce Killers	General Missionary Board	103
Florencia's Uncle	Naomi Thorsen	106

Rhodesia and Malawi
Tambo	R. J. Jacobs	109
Warm Days at Lundi	Beth Beckelhymer	112
We Saw the Pawpaw Trees	Beth Beckelhymer	115

Rwanda
    Spared for Service .... Marti Ensign   117

South Africa
    Practical Points from Pondoland J. W. Haley   119
    African Patriarch Passes ...... J. W. Haley   123
    Encounter with a Lion .... Trygvar Brauteseth   126

Taiwan
    Miracle Church .... Mary Taylor Previte   128

Zaire
    From Shoemaker to Translator   Gerald Bates   134
    The Five-Mile Ladder .... Gerald Bates   139

PREFACE

Every year the Free Methodist Publishing House publishes at least one book focusing on a particular Free Methodist mission field. Several months ago the thought came, Why not put together a book that treated not just one country but all the countries where Free Methodist missionaries are serving. It would provide an overview of what God is doing around the world through Free Methodist missions.

But who could write such a book? No one person is able to represent all eighteen fields. Then why not have various missionaries and nationals write about their own experiences? It occurred to us that this is exactly what has been done throughout the years in the *Missionary Tidings,* official organ of the Woman's Missionary Society. We could publish a variety of articles from past issues of the magazine.

The idea drew enthusiastic endorsement from both the General Missionary Board and the Woman's Missionary Society. Soon former editor, Alice Fensome, was going through stacks and stacks of back issues of the *Tidings,* looking for the "cream of the crop."

A wide assortment of possibilities was then passed around for further evaluation and selection. Finally, the process was completed and forty-two stories remained. Minimal editing was done to keep the articles in their original published form. The titles remain the same. Chapters were arranged alphabetically according to country. Every field is represented at least once.

Taken together the stories provide a powerful

witness to God's love and faithfulness. The book abounds with faith, sacrifice, humor, and a host of other insights into Free Methodist missions. For many years it will provide inspiration for both young and old.

Thank you Alice Fensome, for your many hours of research. And thank you, Leona Fear, Esther Ford, Marian Groesbeck, Robert Haslam, and Charles Kirkpatrick for helping in the selection process.

And thank you, Dorothy Clarke, for designing such an attractive cover.

— G. Roger Schoenhals
Light and Life Press

INTRODUCTION
by Charles D. Kirkpatrick
General Missionary Secretary
of the Free Methodist Church of North America

The past thirty years has been a dynamic period in Free Methodist missions. The *Yearbook* of 1947 reported a total of 13,973 members in the Free Methodist Church scattered throughout ten foreign mission fields and five home mission fields. Supervision for these foreign and home mission fields was delegated to 122 missionaries under appointment with the General Missionary Board of the Free Methodist Church. Care of the 234 organized churches was primarily the responsibility of 92 ordained national pastors. Twenty years later the number of organized churches had grown to 909 under the care of 267 organized national pastors. Membership had climbed to 49,000 members, located in eighteen overseas conferences and three home fields. The missionary staff increased with 200 missionaries under appointment to these fields.

Today the work of missions is totally related to eighteen foreign mission fields. Home missions work has been assigned to the Department of Evangelistic Outreach. The number of organized churches overseas is now 1,096 with 488 ordained national pastors serving these churches. The total membership of the overseas church now exceeds eighty thousand. However, partly because of stronger national leadership, the number of missionaries serving abroad has been reduced to 170.

Another factor making possible the reduction of missionary personnel overseas is a program called

Volunteers in Service Abroad (VISA). This program includes short-term assignments from six months to two years, summer youth crusades, and action groups which serve abroad from a few weeks to several months. The total number serving under VISA since the initiation of the program shortly before 1967 has reached close to two thousand individuals. This vehicle of exposure to overseas missions for people of all ages is an integral part of missions outreach.

Several other new programs within the last ten years have contributed to the development and growth of the national church. Leadership training programs under TEE (Theological Education by Extension) has been the answer on several of our mission fields in the training of nationals. Concentration on a literature ministry whether through distribution or translation has made great impact in the development of the overseas church.

Many of our missionaries, thrust out of mainland China in 1949, were able to establish a foothold in such countries as the Philippines and Taiwan out of which full-fledged conferences were developed.

Evangelistic efforts as well as mergers made in Haiti, Zaire, and Indonesia have brought thousands of persons into membership in the Free Methodist Church abroad. The merger of the Holiness Movement Church with the Free Methodist Church brought under our missionary board the Egypt mission field which has 90 churches and 7,000 members.

The focus of missions since 1967 has been on evangelism and church planting. The cutting edge of missions is reflected by the fact that 70 percent of the missionaries under appointment are working in Bible schools, literature ministries, conference evangelism, and evangelistic projects. The other 30 percent are involved in education, medicine, building skills, and secretarial and bookkeeping positions related to institutions.

In a recent survey covering a growth period of twenty-five years (1947 to 1973), the total growth in membership overseas was 49,593. Of this number 15,802 have been received through merger, leaving 33,711 members related to the evangelistic efforts to the church.

In 1947 there were 556 Sunday schools with an average attendance of 17,965. In 1977 we have 1,057 Sunday schools with an average attendance of 55,109.

Today our ministry extends to six hospitals, eighteen clinics, nine secondary schools, and one junior college. The training program for prospective ministers and potential leaders is carried out through seventeen Bible schools and seminaries which we operate or with which we cooperate.

The stories in this book will make these growth statistics come alive to you as you observe the results of the work and life of some of these wonderful dedicated brothers and sisters, whether nationals or missionaries.

Many stories in this book will reflect how dreams were used to lead some of God's choice people to do exploits for Him — stories like "We Saw the Pawpaw Trees," "God Spoke to Them in a Dream," or "An Encounter with a Lion."

You will smile at the special and unusual experiences of missionaries and nationals as contained in the articles, "Cow in the Clinic," or the struggles of "Victor," known as "Yellow Bear III," a prizefighter who became a fighter for truth and righteousness. Masterpieces of God's power are demonstrated in such stories as "Love Conquers Fierce Killers," "Spared for Service," and "Undefeatable." There are stories of answered prayer, faith that moved mountains, love that replaced hate, good that overcame evil, and hope that reached beyond the grave.

This exciting anthology of missions will provide you with tears and laughter and with praise to God. It will bring you close to the courage, the commitment, and the vision of some remarkable people whom God used for His honor and glory.

BRAZIL
MISSIONARY WITHOUT FURLOUGH
by Beth Smith

SOME people enrich the lives of everyone they meet. One such person is the Rev. Jose Emerenciano of Sao Paulo, Brazil. Perhaps you *did* meet him at the World Cavalcade of Missions in 1969. He was the one dressed in leather as a Brazilian gaucho!

One month after graduation from language study, my husband was appointed as interim pastor of a Brazilian church with Mr. Emerenciano as his assistant. We had first worked with him and his family in 1966 when we were members of the VISA team, and his daughter Cleide was our interpreter. What valuable insights into the Brazilian culture and church he and his wife, Dona Irene, shared with us!

Now, after forty-three years of pastoring, Mr. Emerenciano is retiring. The story of his life encompasses the entire history of the Free Methodist mission in Brazil, for he has worked beside all our missionaries — from the beginning until now. He has literally been a "missionary without furlough." Join us in the living room of his new home as he tells this story.

"After my conversion in 1923, in the interior of northern Brazil, I had to leave my home because of the conflict with my family who wanted me to return to Catholicism. I received God's call to be a minister. Without resources it was difficult to study, but God opened doors to seminary and university training. I wanted to be well prepared to do His work.

"I was invited to Japan to study the language and customs for two years, and there I met the Rev. T. Tsuchiyama and the Rev. E. E. Shelhamer of the Free Methodist Church. Soon after returning to Brazil to work with the Japanese of the Holiness Church, I met the Rev. Daniel Nishizumi, a man with a dream. He wanted to begin a Free Methodist work among the Japanese in Brazil.

"In 1939 Bishop Ormston, Byron Lamson, and Mr. Shelhamer arrived to survey the prospects of beginning a mission and seminary. After World War II when Lucile Damon and Helen Voller arrived as the first missionaries, Dona Irene and I began helping them.

"Suddenly Daniel Nishizumi died in an auto accident and we faced a great moment of decision. But we put ourselves in God's hands, came to Sao Paulo with heavy hearts, and in our home, in 1948, began the first Free Methodist church in Brazil.

"More missionaries came and the church grew. The Japanese and Brazilians worshiped together, and Brazil became a Provisional Conference connected to the Pacific Coast Japanese Conference.

"God blessed this work with a great spirit of prayer, and one answer was received when Spring Arbor College sent money to buy land for a seminary. So the dream of Daniel Nishizumi became a reality."

Later, at a farewell service, the Rev. Jose Emerenciano stated, "I hope that my life, as Paul's did, will encourage others to live fully dedicated to Christ." And it has!

After pastoring a number of Brazilian and Japanese churches, he has been responsible for directing the lives of many young people into Christian service. People of all ages have responded to his warm personal interest. Troubled hearts have opened to him in confidence for scripture, prayer, and counsel.

Our Free Methodist mission in Brazil owes much to this man who speaks Japanese, English, and Portuguese fluently, and who bridges cultural and generation gaps in Christ-like love.

— Dateline: October, 1973

BRAZIL

GOD SPOKE TO THEM IN A DREAM
by G. Lucile Damon Ryckman

A few weeks ago we were invited to Sunday dinner in the home of one of the dentists who is a member of our Sao Paulo church. One of the other guests was Dr. Hiroyuki Hayashi, also a dentist and one of our local deacons. After dinner, while we were sitting on the verandah enjoying the blue sky and white clouds of a lovely autumn day, we said, "Brother Hayashi, now is a good time for you to tell us about your conversion and call to Brazil. We have heard snatches of the story, but we want to know all of it."

And so this humble "fisher of men" told us, partly in English and partly in Portuguese, the following story:

"When I was a child in Japan I went occasionally to a Christian Sunday school, though my parents were pagans. At the age of sixteen, while attending a Christian meeting, I felt a great desire to give my heart to Christ, but did not because of the influence of a friend.

"A short time after this, my favorite sister, who was a Christian, died, then my cousin and later my mother. As a result, I began to think about death, from whence I came, where I was going, what I was. Becoming exceedingly melancholy, I tried to find relief in sports.

"Then I went to Osaka to study dentistry. My leisure hours there were spent in sports, dancing, and drinking in an effort to escape from the increasing inner conflict and torment. In the depths of despair, I remembered again my Christian sister, who had died with a victorious faith. But, filled with fears, I was unwilling to yield myself to Christianity.

"Shortly after this, as I was walking along the street one evening, I thought I saw this sister standing among a group of people. Eagerly and quickly I drew near, but instead of my sister I found a gospel street meeting. As I listened to the preaching, my heart was suddenly broken, and with tears I sought and found salvation. Not long afterward I became acquainted with the Free Methodist Church and was baptized in 1929 by Rev. T. Kawabe.

"After I graduated from the dental school, in 1930, I moved to Kobe. There I had a great struggle with inbred sin. When Rev. E. E. Shelhamer came to Kobe the following year, I attended three of his meetings and heard clearly explained the way of sanctification. After six months of earnest seeking, I obtained the experience. Soon after this God called me to preach. In 1932 I returned to the land of my birth where I married a Christian young woman whose mother and grandmother were also Christians.

"On New Year's night of 1933 I had a dream of a broad, wide land with many eucalyptus trees. Many Japanese were there. Sitting under the shade of a tree a little distance away, I watched them. I was very hungry, but there was nothing for me to eat. Then Jesus came and handed me a package. Opening it, I found only a skull and bones, and then I awoke. I reached for my watch to see the time. My wife, too, was awake and asked, 'What is the matter?' As I told her of my dream, she listened with amazement and said, 'I have just now had the *very same dream!* What can it mean?'

"For a year we could not forget the dream, and yet neither of us understood the significance of it. I was practicing dentistry and on weekends was giving my time to the directing of three Sunday schools. One winter day when my wife and I were in my office, I received a letter from my younger brother, who was not well and was desiring to go to another country. As I read it I remembered that he had at one time talked about going to Brazil. The minute 'Brazil' came to my mind, I said to my wife, 'Brazil! Do you suppose our dream meant Brazil? But Brazil is a land of coffee trees, and we saw eucalyptus.'

"While we were warming our hands over the stove and discussing the subject, in walked one of our friends who was a Christian evangelist. When we told him of our dream and present conversation, he said, 'Why, Brother Hayashi, that is Amazonas in northern Brazil where there is a Japanese colony.'

"After praying about it, we felt that we should present our names to the company which was sending colonists to Brazil. Usually no colonists were accepted unless they had some sons old enough to work, and we had only one baby girl, Sumiko. But in a few weeks the representative of the company told us, 'We need a dentist in Amazonas and we want you to go.'

"In 1934 we arrived in Amazonas. The colony was so small that within three months I had treated every person there. In the hot, unhealthful climate all of us became ill with malaria. After our recovery we felt the Lord directing us to move to Sao Paulo, and so here we are today. The scene of our dream has become reality, not only in regard to the eucalyptus trees but also in respect to the many Japanese people spiritually starving for the gospel of our Lord Jesus Christ."

Through the week Dr. Hayashi works long hours in his dental laboratory in the city, but weekends are filled with work for the Master. He holds regular "cottage meetings" on Saturday nights and Sunday afternoons, goes on frequent evangelistic trips to the interior, preaches once each month in Janira, helps in the young people's work, and is assistant pastor of the Sao Paulo Japanese church. Without stint he gives to the Kingdom of his total resources — material, physical, and spiritual — and is truly fulfilling the call of God as a missionary among the 500,000 Japanese people in the state of Sao Paulo.

— Dateline: December, 1947

BURUNDI
Cow in the Clinic
by Doris Moore

OUR clinic program in Muyebe to assist in the feeding of Burundi children who have a protein deficiency disease has been excitingly worthwhile. It began as a faith venture. So many children who came past my clinic desk had the red hair and swollen abdomen typical of the disease. I was busy and argued that I didn't have time to do anything about it, but it finally "got to me."

In three weeks my pilot project ballooned into a full-blown program. I had a supply of beans and powdered milk but it was soon gone. Then I was faced with the problem of the need of a new supply, and no finances.

I went to a Catholic relief organization sponsored by United States A.I.D. money. I felt that as an American mission in Burundi we were entitled to their supplies if we could prove our project worthwhile.

After their investigation they said we were eligible. So I drove to their headquarters in a VW pickup truck. When they saw the truck they said, "You want more food than that, don't you?"

"Sure," I said, "I'll take all I can get." We loaded the pickup and went home.

Then I went to look at trucks. The man had said to bring a big one so I selected a seven-ton truck and sent the driver to the warehouse for supplies. The Lord said "Ask largely," didn't He?

Three days later we had seven tons of powdered eggs, powdered milk, oil, wheat, corn flour, white flour, and other wonderful protein foods. Just a few days later the entire program was frozen and not another thing was distributed for months. But we had food and in two or three weeks we could see the reddish hair begin to turn black.

Three days a week parents brought their children to the clinic. For three hours they sat and waited while the children were fed. I decided they could help in the project by bringing their hoes and working in the garden, so I planted soybeans.

The parents were so proud to be helping. They got strings to lay out straight rows and had a beautiful garden. They were so proud of it that they wanted the government agriculturists to see it.

The inspectors were quite impressed. "Where did you get the seed?" they asked.

"I bought it at a certain agency and paid twenty-five cents a kilo for it."

"Well," they said, "you're feeding the children, and this is a state-sponsored program so we will pay for the seed."

So here we were with all kinds of seed and a double plot of soybeans. It was no longer my program — it was theirs. We got two 55-gallon drums of beans off the first crop.

After carrying on the program for some months, I decided I should get out and see the people in their villages so I scheduled a visit to three homes.

I bought an old bicycle with hand brakes and finally learned to ride it. One day I started out with an African friend, for I was afraid I might get lost in the bush if I went alone. We took a little jar of baby food for each child.

The first home we visited was poor. There was no chair to sit on, but the ground had been swept clean to prepare for our coming. We played with the children and had a wonderful time.

After prayer I started to leave. At the time I was unaware that in Burundi, when one schedules a visit to a home, it is polite for the host or hostess to give a gift to the visitor. They came with three eggs. I had been trying to get eggs for months and was delighted with the gift.

But all at once I remembered the uphill-downhill roads and the hand brakes on my bike. I looked at my African friend thinking, *How am I going to get these eggs home?*

He must have read my thoughts because he walked to a banana tree, pulled off a leaf, and tore it in half. He put the two strips at right angles in my palm, put the eggs in the middle, and tied the bundle with a piece of fiber. I clutched the eggs in one hand, and hanging to the bike for dear life, started down the road.

At the next home I was given a live chicken! What to do now? My African friend knew. He found a length of inner tubing, tore it into lengths and tied knots in it, and wound it around my baggage carrier. He stuck the chicken under the inner tubing and we went squawking down the road. I collected thirty-six eggs and three live chickens that day. And me steering with one hand!

About four miles before we reached home, someone called to us from a house surrounded by trees. The first thing I saw as we approached the house was a dead cow. I learned that the cow barn had burned down during the night.

In a nearby enclosure there was a cow with a calf. The cow had been badly burned. The owners didn't want to lose both the cow and the calf so they asked me to treat the burns. Not having had veterinary training with my nursing course I said, "I don't have my medical guide with me. If you want to bring the cow in to the clinic tomorrow morning we'll see what we can do to help you."

A cow to the clinic? From four miles out? Of course they wouldn't! But the next morning I looked up from my desk and there was a cow in the clinic line! I wrote "cow" on the ticket, gave it a clinic number, and went to look at it. Then I went back to the pharmacy for a half-pound of antibiotic ointment and rubber gloves. I plastered ointment all over the side of the cow. Then the owners said, "In Africa we don't feel we get treated unless we get a shot."

A shot? For a cow? What kind of shot? But I went back to the pharmacy, mixed up some penicillin and got a needle and syringe. Before I got the needle through the first hair, it broke and penicillin went everywhere. So back to the pharmacy for new equipment and for a second attempt which was successful.

Two weeks after that incident, these people came to church. Three weeks later they were at the altar. And now there are new Christians in Burundi because we took time for something that was important to them.

— Dateline: January-February, 1975

CHINA

SUDDEN DEATH — SUDDEN GLORY
by Mary O. Schlosser

It is a comforting thought that our God is everywhere present, and not one of His little ones is forgotten of Him. Last spring in the terrible siege of Kaifeng, Brother Liu, one of our church members there, had a glorious experience of God's grace. Brother Liu owned a donkey and a little flour mill and sold flour for a living. His clothes were generally floury from his trade and he was not at all a wealthy man. But his consistent Christian life and testimony had won for him the respect of his neighbors.

When the fighting became hotter and the shells were falling all around, some fell on the roof of his house and rolled off without exploding. This fact and also the fact that they knew Brother Liu was a man of prayer made the neighbors feel his court was a safe place to hide. So they poured into the yard and house, getting under the beds and chairs and tables and into every corner.

Our brother recognized in this an opportunity for urging them all to turn to the Lord, and he loudly proclaimed to them the gospel of saving grace. "Don't think this house can protect you," he told them. "We are not promised deliverance from danger in this life. The important thing is for you to repent and be saved from your sins so you can escape the suffering of hell in the world to come." For two days he kept urging the people, and many began to pray as the bombs fell and every moment seemed as if it might be their last.

"On the morning of the third day Brother Liu bathed himself when he arose and to the astonishment of his wife, he proceeded to put on his best clothes. The only explanation he gave was that "God was calling him and now he was ready to go." The day wore on and he was occupied as before in pleading with the people to repent, when suddenly a bomb fell and landed right on his head! He was instantly killed, of course, and his preaching was finished; his work was done.

This event made a great impression for good on the people and is even now having its effect. His wife who was right there and saw it all, was mightily stirred up to follow the Lord more closely. At conference time she witnessed about it to the church full of people. With tears streaming down her face, she described it all and gave the glory to God that He should so have prepared His servant and used him at the last.

— Dateline: January, 1949

CHINA

THE LORD'S MESSENGER
by James H. Taylor

THE edict for the destruction of the Christians in China had gone forth from Peking, and in some sections of the country was being followed out with barbarous cruelty. The massacres were almost more terrible in the province of Shansi than in any other.

Mr. and Mrs. Wang, simple farmers in Shansi, were devoted Christians. Long before the trouble actually broke out, there had been persistent rumors. The social atmosphere all over the countryside as it related particularly to the Christians, was ominous with impending tragedy. The Wangs prayed constantly for guidance. They lived in a small home in a country village. After much prayer they were led to leave their home for the mountains, a day's journey away where there were many empty cave dwellings.

While hiding there they continued in prayer that they might know what next to do. A misstep might mean death, either if they stayed too long or if they left too soon.

One day the woman was sitting under a tree earnestly praying for direction, when a bird flew into the branches. This bird visits Shansi annually and its note sounds like, "K'uai k'uai chong ku, K'uai k'uai chong ku," repeated several times. But today its note sounded different — it said, "K'uai k'uai chia ch'u, K'uai k'uai chia ch'u," over and over again. The woman listened intently. Had God sent a bird to deliver a message? Was He using this means to answer their prayers? So Mr. Wang interpreted it when his wife related the incident to him. They immediately prepared to leave for home, for "chia" means "home," and the bird had so clearly repeated "Hasten home," there could be no misunderstanding the message.

But there were two possible roads. Which were they to take, the north or the south? The dangers of those days were terrible. So again they prayed and were directed to follow the North road. Thus they arrived safely that night back again in their village home.

Their acquaintances were astonished. "How did you get back without mishap?" they asked in amazement. In reply they related how the Lord had been with them and had so strangely guided them in answer to prayer. Then they heard of the dangers unknown to them from which God had so remarkably delivered them.

The day before a band of boxers had come to their home to kill them, and had found it empty. Someone in the village told the boxers where the Christians were hiding, so after spending the night there, they started off in the morning by the southern road on their nefarious errand, only to find on their arrival that the mountain cave was empty. The Lord's messenger, the little harvest bird, had been there before them.

Shortly after this incident an edict came from Peking that Christians were not to be further molested, so these two godly people lived on in peace, fearlessly witnessing to the truth of the gospel, and to the fact that Jesus answers prayer.

— Dateline: May, 1947

CHINA

The Power of a Bible
by Alice Hayes Taylor

"Ding! Ding! Dong! Ding! Dong!" clanged the brass cymbal that announced that the seller of peanuts, candy, and watermelon seeds was passing by.

"Mother, give me some money to buy some salted peanuts," shouted Sin Min as he ran breathlessly into his yard from the street.

"Why must you spend so much money for knick knacks every day?" scolded his mother. "It is not right for a child to want so much."

But when he continued his coaxing and teasing, she yielded to him and gave him the money, for he was her only son. In a few minutes he returned to his own yard to eat the peanuts, for if he remained along the street to eat them it would be necessary for him to share them with his little friends with whom he had been playing. When he finished them, he threw the piece of paper in which the peanuts had been wrapped onto the ground and rejoined his friends at play.

Some time later Sin Min's father, Mr. Wang, returned home from work, and walking into the yard, saw a piece of paper with printed words on it lying there. Picking it up he read it and found that it related the story of one who did many good deeds and who said that he was the Son of God; but his friends did not believe him and wanted to kill him.

"Where did this paper come from?" he asked Sin Min's mother. "Where is the rest of the book? This is a wonderful story, and I want to read all of it and find out how it ends."

"Sin Min brought it in with his peanuts wrapped in it," she replied. "I don't know where he got it. Ask him, and perhaps he can help you find the rest of the book."

Walking to the front gate, Mr. Wang called to Sin Min, who was playing on the street, "Sin Min, come here. I want to ask you something."

The boy came running, wondering what he had done that was wrong.

"Where did you get this sheet of paper?" asked the father. "I want to read the rest of the story."

"I bought it from the peanut vendor this afternoon," he replied.

"Where is he now?" asked the father. "Take me to him."

Together they walked down the street for several blocks, and soon on a side street they could hear the ding-dong of the vendor.

"There he is," shouted Sin Min. "That is the man."

"Whey Whey!" called Mr. Wang to the vendor, who turned quickly, hoping to make a sale.

"What book is this that you are using to wrap your peanuts?" asked the father.

"I bought the book," was the puzzled reply of the vendor. "I did not steal it." He feared that he was being suspected of theft.

"Let me see the book," said Mr. Wang. "I want to see how the story ends."

But he soon discovered that the vendor had made many sales since Sin Min bought his peanuts, and the main part of the story was gone.

"Where did you buy the book?" asked Mr. Wang. "I must buy one."

"Let me take you to the man who sold it to me," said the vendor.

Some blocks away they came to a courtyard where lived a man who had become poor and was selling off his books to meet expenses.

"Have you more books like this one?" asked Mr. Wang. "I want to get one so that I can finish the story."

"No," was the reply. "That is the only one I

had. My son got it as a prize at the Christian Sunday school. I have read only a little of it, and now that I need money more than books, I sold it to this man for a small sum. It is cheaper to use it to wrap his wares than any other paper he can buy."

"Where can I get one?" asked Mr. Wang.

"Down at the Christian church two blocks from here," he replied. Again Mr. Wang went in search of the book with a wonderful story. The pastor of the church was only too glad to sell him a copy of the Bible and to explain the meaning of the story. Mr. Wang not only read his Bible but also went to church services. It was not long before he and his entire family became Christians.

— Dateline: September, 1948

CHINA

THE PROVIDENTIAL GIFT
by E.P. Ashcraft

DURING the Japanese invasion of China practically all the colleges and universities, as well as many of the middle schools, migrated to the far west. Many of them trekked overland carrying books, clothing, and even pieces of furniture.

Finding a new location in which to continue their work was not always easy. Many of the students and teachers suffered from diseases of various kinds, partly due to exposure or to malnutrition. But those who knew God found that he did not fail them. Miracles were wrought during those years of testing which reminded one of God's care for Israel in the Wilderness.

The following incident was told me while crossing the Pacific recently by a Methodist Principal of one of these schools, who had had several hundred students under his care. They had traveled for hundreds of miles and at last located in a village not far from Chungking. Buildings were quite adequate, but the water supply was not only unhealthful, due to the fact of the wells being shallow, but also very limited. Many people of the district were consulted, but all said it would be impossible to find good water in the neighborhood, for it had been tried too many times without success.

But water must be found from some source. "After much prayer," said Principal Hsiung, "I felt led to go out into the school yard to a certain spot and draw a circle several feet in diameter. In the center of this I made a cross, to mark the place for the well."

People laughed. "Why spend your money so foolishly?" The proposition seemed so unwise that it was difficult to find men who would work on the job. The whole district seemed to be underlaid with rock which cropped out on the surface in many places. Men were at last secured, however, and work was begun with hammer and chisel. The well was large enough to permit two or three of them to labor at the same time.

For four months they drilled away, but no water. They had gone down forty feet. Some criticized. Some became discouraged. The workmen wished to quit. Consultation. Earnest prayer. "What is the use? Four months and no water.

Let's quit."

"No, I believe this is the place God told us to dig," said the man of faith. "Let us keep digging in faith."

Three more months added another thirty feet, but still no water. The discouragement and criticism increased, and more earnest prayer, agonizing prayer followed, with deepening conviction in the heart of Principal Hsiung that God would answer — with water.

So, the hammering continued until one morning, just as the people were gathering for worship, a man came running, calling as he ran, "Water! Water! Water! There's water in the well." Everyone was excited and ran to the well to see for themselves.

Sure enough one of the masons had accidentally struck the side of the well with his chisel and had tapped an underground stream. The water poured in with such rapidity that the men had to be pulled quickly to the surface, and in their haste, abandoned their tools. Within a few minutes the water was ten feet deep, and by an hour or more it had risen thirty feet. There it found its level and stopped.

Water, indeed! And the best of water! Sufficient not only for the school, but an ample supply for the entire village. Regardless of how much was taken out, the level remained the same. Later, when other wells failed because of the drought, the "prayer well" continued with its abundant supply. Far and wide people recognized that God had answered the prayer of the Christians.

Do you wonder that Principal Hsiung and his co-workers, when dedicating the well, gave it the name, "The Providential Gift of God to Co-sufferers"? Not only had the well quenched the thirst of thousands but it also had brought the opportunity to tell many of the Water of Life.

— Dateline: January, 1948

CHINA

THEY CALLED — GOD ANSWERED
by Alice Hayes Taylor

ONE year after our return to China following our last furlough, war broke out between China and Japan. In another year our field in Honan was occupied by Japanese troops, and in still another year we were driven from our home by anti-foreign demonstrations. We waited at the coast where our four children were in school, hoping that conditions would clear up and we could return to our work, only to find matters becoming worse and worse. These were months of earnest waiting upon God to make His will known. Should we return to America with the children, or should we leave the children at school in enemy-occupied territory at the coast and answer the calls coming from Chinese Christians to open a new work in China's needy Northwest? Gradually God made it clear to us that He wanted us to go to the Northwest and leave the children at the coast. (Since there are no English-speaking schools in the interior it is necessary for parents to place their children in schools at the coast.)

Although this was two years before Pearl

Harbor we could see that war between Japan and United States was inevitable. Our first thoughts were of the children, for missionaries are also human. When war broke out all enemy subjects would, as a matter of course, be interned in a concentration camp, and with the raping of Nanking and other cities fresh in our minds, our hearts recoiled from it. How could we entertain the thought of leaving our children six hundred miles from us in enemy hands?

Just at that time God gave us Matthew 6:33, "Seek ye first the kingdom of God and His righteousness and all these things shall be added unto you," couched in the words of a former aged pastor, "Look after the things dear to God, and He will look after those dear to you." Who were those dear to God? The souls in Northwest China to whom He was calling us. Who were those dear to us? The four children separated from us by warring lines.

Confident that God would fulfill His promise we bade farewell to the children, the youngest of whom was just six years old and the oldest just twelve. In a remarkable way God led us through enemy territory, across the front lines into Free China and then on to Northwest China where we labored one and a half years before Pearl Harbor. We started the Northwest Bible Institute, and opened several new stations.

Then one day the Chinese newspaper flashed bold headlines of Pearl Harbor. Hastily we scanned the columns and knew that America was at war with Japan. You may imagine our heart anguish as we realized that our four children with hundreds of others were in Japanese hands as enemy prisoners. We quickly sought the quiet of our bedroom and with deep emotion cried to God, our Refuge, to protect the children. After some time God caused our emotions to subside and then spoke, "When you made the decision to leave the children at the coast and come here to the Northwest, did I not tell you to 'look after those dear to me and I'd look after those dear to you' "?

"Yes," I replied through my tears.

"Just keep on caring for those dear to me and I'll keep on caring for those dear to you," came the comforting voice of God. With that He wiped the tears from our eyes and filled us with fresh courage. In the four years that followed as we went from place to place holding meetings and helping to pray people into the Kingdom, He took away all anxiety for the welfare of the children.

How did God answer?

1. Japanese guards did not molest any of the people interned in that camp.

2. During those years when the children were interned, China saw one of the worst famines of her history in which thousands of Chinese starved to death. It would have been a small thing for the Japanese to starve or kill enemy internees, especially when they were having difficulty to get enough food for their armies. But God prevented it, and though the food was insufficient and of an inferior quality, it was enough to sustain life.

3. When Communists prevented grain from coming from the interior to Japanese occupied territory, the Japanese moved the concentration camp back of the Communist lines so that the internees could have grain.

4. Though the children were thin when the war was over, there is nothing organically wrong with any of them.

5. The Northwest Bible Institute has averaged over fifty young men and women in training for the ministry. Some have already entered the Lord's work.

6. Outside of the Bible School seven regular preaching places have been opened in the Northwest.

— Dateline: June, 1947

CHINA

FAMILY REUNION
by Alice Hayes Taylor

SEPTEMBER 11, 1945 was one of the happiest days of our lives. We were just preparing to sit down about 7:30 in the evening for a faculty meeting. Some of the members of the faculty had already arrived when we heard a commotion in the darkness outside our window, and almost immediately our door opened, and a Chinese in excited tones announced, "The children have arrived." In astonishment I inquired, "What children?" never thinking of our four coming in over a dangerous road, through the rain and mud after dark. Before my question could be answered, the thin face of Mary appeared in the door, followed by John, James, and Kathleen. As we all tried to throw our arms around each other at the same time, and tears of joy started, Kathleen whispered to me "John is sick, and we had to carry him in part of the way."

American airmen had brought them from the

concentration camp at Weihsien to Sian, one hundred thirty miles from here, by plane. The Japanese had made an airfield near the camp, so that the children had a trip of only about eight miles from the concentration camp to the airfield by truck. In four hours they were in Sian where the American officers gave them a fine welcome party, finishing off with a frosted cake with the word "welcome" written across the top. They took a picture of the party by flashlight and later sent us a copy. Mr. Taylor had arranged with the officers at the airfield to turn the children over to Mr. Song, the Chinese Christian who took us into his home when we first came to Shensi five years ago, and he would bring them on by train to us. This would get them here almost two days earlier than if they waited to let us know they had arrived and then waited for us to come and get them.

Mr. Song phoned ahead to the railway station where they were to get off, and had horse carts hired and waiting to bring them the last sixteen miles overland, as soon as the train got into the station. By doing this they were able to come right on home without any delay and get here the same day. There was a slow rain when they got off the train, and the roads were muddy so that the animals crept along slowly. It was far too slow a pace for four active children who had not seen their parents for five and a half years, so after they had sat for a few miles on a jolting cart, they got down and walked, or ran. They did not know the way, and they had forgotten most of their Chinese but as they ran along through the mud, they kept asking where Fengsiang was. Mary and John were wet and chilled through, so the two older children took off their sweaters and gave them to them.

John was sick to begin with, and with the cold and overfatigue combined with the excitement, he gave out and could not walk any farther. Then Kathleen and Jamie took turns carrying him until a Chinese cart came along and took him on and led them to within a block or two of where we live. They had inquired of Chinese who were passing where Mr. Taylor lived and found one who could lead them to our gate. One of the students then led them back to our house. We took them into our bedroom, got warm water, and washed the mud from their bare legs and feet, after which we tucked John into a pair of his daddy's pajamas and put him into our bed while we helped the others to wash off the mud. They were so excited and tired that they ate very little food the first night, but the next day they began to eat. At the noon meal John looked at me and asked, "Mamma, can we eat all we want?" When I replied that there were no restrictions, they held back no longer, and I tell you we have tucked away quantities of food in the last three weeks.

John and Mary were the thinnest of all. In the first week they all put on weight, but John headed the list with five pounds. They craved fresh fruit more than anything else and got here just as the persimmons were beginning to ripen. Kathleen and Jamie seem very well, but John and Mary seem to have little reserve so we have not assigned them much work. Mary has a peculiar cough which they diagnosed at the camp as asthma, but we want an X-ray soon, to see if it is anything more serious. Jamie carries the water every day; Mary and Kathleen lay the table and wash dishes;

John carries off the garbage and carries the milk to and from the cellar. They tend to their own rooms and do most of the washing and ironing. Kathleen is also helping with the sewing.

Fortunately I had made them some new clothes before they got out of camp, guessing at the sizes. It is practically all they have that is suitable for wear here. The girls' skirts are way above their knees and they have only anklets or no socks. They have an old pair of shoes each, and the U.S. forces gave the boys each a pair of long pants far too large, and a pair of calf-skin shoes, also too big. I had supposed that of course the Red Cross would be there with clothing for these refugees as soon as the war was over, but not a stitch did they provide. The U.S. Army treated them as war prisoners and dropped by parachute men's clothing and food supplies. It was providential that we were unable to sell off much of our cloth material when we had so many alarms that the Japanese were coming on here and we would have to evacuate. I am now making it up into clothing for the children. This all takes time, and with my classes in the Bible Training School and the duties in the church and home, I have little time for sewing.

It is a good thing that we did not know all the dangers to which they were exposed. I had been apprehensive of the treatment the Japanese might give the older girls, but there was no reason for fear along that line. How we thank God that our four have been kept clean.

The four have developed very much. Kathleen is a real homemaker who wants things tidy. She is very much interested in her appearance. Jamie is very strong and sees things to do. He comes along and says, "Mother, let me do that. While I'm here,

I'm not seeing you lift heavy things." Mary and John are interested in music. Mary had a little, six years ago, enough to give her a taste, and I have just started John. All our music books were lost, so I have to write all their exercises for them, and does it keep me busy! They want pretty tunes. All four of them sing well in parts. Kathleen and Mary make fine alto harmony and Jamie is developing a deep bass voice, while John is trying tenor and keeps to his part with my assistance. They sang "Rock of Ages" in parts at the Y.P.M.S., the first Saturday they were here.

— Dateline: February, 1946

DOMINICAN REPUBLIC
A Dominican Pastor
by Rachel M. Smiley

YEARS ago a six foot angular fellow named Luis Maria King was given a scholarship at the Instituto Evangelico. He wanted to prepare for the ministry. He wasn't very promising but he had been persistent in asking. Like most of our scholarship students, he had had only five years of schooling. Though a young man he had to take his place with children in the school.

As the years went by he proved his worth. He took responsibility, developed in leadership and was a great help during vacations to the pastors where he worked as an evangelist. His good humor won him friends everywhere.

After graduating from the Theological Department in 1946 he served as assistant pastor for the remainder of the year. At Conference he was appointed to the circuit of Monte Christy. He married and moved to his new circuit. It was a big change for he went from the rainy eastern end of the island to the extreme western part of the Dominican Republic which has scarcely any rainfall.

A month later he entertained the District Quarterly Meeting. We were interested in seeing how he and his wife were adjusting to their new life and work. I had a special interest as they had both been students in the school. Chela had been with me in the girls' dormitory for three years. Luis had spent seven or eight years at the school. We had worked, studied and prayed together. Many times he had talked with me about his problems and desire to be useful in the Lord's work.

Luis and Chela welcomed me on our arrival. "You are our mother and this is your home. You must ask for anything you want." When I demurred saying I expected to fare like the rest, they insisted that I was to have anything I wanted. Each night thereafter they had something special saved for me.

It was Sunday afternoon. When I entered the parsonage, Luis said supper wasn't ready and asked me to go for a little walk. As we walked along the dusty streets he unburdened his heart and mind to me. Adding emphasis with his hands the words came tumbling over each other. There were many and difficult problems in the church. "I want to do things the right way and be as efficient as possible. You are my mother and mothers are supposed to tell us our faults. I want you to look around and notice all my mistakes. When you go home you write me your criticisms and I shall try to correct my errors." The utter sincerity and humility were touching. I assured him I thought he was doing a good job. I tried to explain that mothers should encourage as well as criticize.

Last summer I received a letter from Luis. He wrote:

"We now have an eight month old boy called Luis Emilio. We have just had the Y.P.M.S. Regional here with much success. I have been ordained. How many blessings the Lord has given me! I weigh 198 pounds and am a giant. My circuit is progressing much. What I am lacking is something in which to travel. I do not have a horse and a donkey is too small 'y no me resiste.' Pray that the Lord will provide me a motorcycle. I can assure you that my circuit soon will not be the smallest as there is a hunger for the Gospel. Many times I am so sad because I cannot do the work with all my ardor or rather according to my calling as I have always told you and I see the world miserable, sad and agonizing, and all for lack of God. This arid dry region is my world and I want to go to this world with the truth of Christ. But how can I go? In what? You can understand my condition. I tell you I am doing all I can as far as I can reach. Doesn't it seem to you that as I am young and strong I could go farther and do better? Yes, pray for me."

Yes, I can understand his condition. His circuit has many points widely separated. I remember the long dry dusty road from Santiago to Monte Cristy, a region of catcus and desert growth. Goats are common for few other animals can subsist there. One is surprised to see an occasional house and several villages. How can the people exist? Where do they get their water? How do they make a living? Stranger yet, these villages have great crowds on market days when the people from the surrounding mountainous regions gather to sell their produce and buy necessities for their families.

What a circuit to try to travel! An overcrowded bus goes from Monte Cristy to Santiago once a day. With the loss of much time the villages on the highway can be reached. What about those other places back in the mountains? A horse would starve to death. A donkey would be easier to care for here but what a slow means of travel and as Luis says they could not "resist" him. I can see him on a donkey, his feet dragging on the ground or jack-knifed under him. Roads reach to all parts of his circuit. A motorcycle would enable him to do two or three times the work he can do now.

My heart rejoiced ever since I heard a motorcycle was on the way to the Dominican Republic.

— Dateline: May, 1949

EGYPT
UNDEFEATABLE FAITH
by Norman E. Cooke

I walked in front of the Rev. Labeeb Ateyah's funeral procession, with its gilded, glass-sided carriage drawn by eight robed and hooded horses, along with ministers representing many denominations, and a choir of laymen. We walked around several city blocks while the choir sang hymns of conquering faith.

Many followed the procession which halted at his church in Shubra, Cairo, where he had been a pastor for the past eight years. Only a fraction of the crowd was able to squeeze into the church. The others crowded doorways or sat in the huge tapestry tent set up in the street beside the church for the mourners.

It was hard to see Labeeb Ateyah's widow and seven children mourn the loss of their loved one. Yet the funeral service had a note of victory in the seven speeches given and in the joyful tears of listeners. A life of undefeatable faith had gained its final triumph.

Labeeb Ateyah, since his birth in 1915, had come a long way from the humble home of a village carpenter in upper Egypt. But this humble home in Salamone was one of the secret's of Labeeb's successful life.

"My greatest heritage," wrote Labeeb, "was that I was born of Christian parents. Our house was near the church which I attended from the time I was born until I was nineteen years old. Even though I was not 'born again,' my mother insisted on my attendance, and I learned Scriptures and hymns."

Labeeb's father had plans for his boy — he saw him in a police officer's uniform, riding on a horse. In order to see his dream come true, he went to Assiut to meet missionary J. C. Black of the Canadian Holiness Movement Church. The Rev. Mr. Black promised to do his best, when he met the chief of police in Cairo, to obtain Labeeb's entrance into Police College. The two men ended their conversation by discussing the great need of the church for educated, born-again young men such as Labeeb.

Ateyah, Labeeb's father, left the mission feeling that God would certainly make his dream come true and see that his son entered the police force. However, on his return to Assiut after a few weeks, he learned to his surprise that the missionary had not presented Labeeb's case before the chief of police in Cairo. Although meeting the chief for another reason, he explained to the astonished father that he did not feel it was God's will that he recommend the son for entrance to Police College.

Labeeb found work with the railroad, settled in Cairo, and began attending the Qollali church, where he was active in the youth group. His talents were quickly spotted, and he was elected president of the society.

As well as holding successful meetings in their own church, the young people were leaders in beginning Sunday schools and meetings in new parts of the city. Labeeb found a faithful, enthusiastic friend in the church. Together he and Abdu Fahmy formed the spiritual foundation for the Babadublu church, which has been established since 1950.

Labeeb began to plan his life's pattern. He would marry and, along with his friend Abdu, he would work in Cairo, serving God and opening new churches. He felt the pull to full-time service as a pastor, but at the same time he wanted to help his brothers become educated and bring them to Cairo to find work. All these ideas he made known to his family in the south, except the urging of the Holy Spirit toward the ministry. His future plans pleased his parents, but one day a letter came that dashed his father's dreams and brought tears to his mother's eyes.

Labeeb wrote, "I was walking along the street, when suddenly I was buried under a wagonload of heavy logs. Shrieks arose from the people standing near, and everyone pitched in to uncover my body from the logs. When they found me unhurt and able to speak, thanking them for their help, they were much astonished, for they expected to find a lifeless body. Smiling, I left them and went to my room to write you that I have obeyed God's will and plan to enter the ministry."

As Labeeb's youngest brother read this letter to his parents, he was aware of their disappointment. They said, "Our son will become a pastor and be moved from village to village."

At that critical moment, missionary Black entered the house in Salamone. He, too, had received a letter from young Labeeb asking that he be assigned to a church. He told Labeeb's parents that he had already stationed their son at Kom Buha.

When he sensed the father's disappointment, he hugged him and told him this was God's will and that God had answered prayers and not dreams. After prayer, the parents also surrendered to God's will for their son.

One of Labeeb Ateyah's early pastorates was in the town of Masra. When he arrived in the town, none of the brethren came to meet him or help him with his furniture. More than that, none came to worship in the church. They had had a bad experience with a former pastor and were ashamed to be associated with the church.

It was a real blow to the young pastor and his

wife, but they prayed much and continued to be friendly. After some time, the people began to attend church. It was not too long until a good revival broke out, and some young men who were saved in the revival later entered the ministry. Labeeb's faith and steadiness in the face of extreme difficulty were richly rewarded.

In the city of Luxor, he found himself, as he described it, "preaching in one of the Pharonic temples," because his old church had about six pillars supporting the roof. "Impossible to build a new church in Luxor," he was told over and over again. Not discouraged, he bought property behind the small church, tore down the old church, and began to build, only to be stopped by authorities who demanded his government decree giving him the right to construct a new church.

Off to Cairo went Labeeb, to be sent from government office to government office trying to get the proper signatures. Finally Labeeb reached the Republican Palace with his request. He left there rejoicing — with the President's signature on his permit.

A missionary asked him, "Do you have money with which to build?" He smiled and answered, "I have the riches of prayer." So with the riches of prayer and the President's signature, the Rev. Labeeb Ateyah built a beautiful new church in the famous city of ancient Thebes, now called Luxor. From Luxor he moved to Cairo, where he also had successful pastorates before he died.

Not only did Labeeb bring revival to dead churches and build new ones, but he also served his conference well. As chairman of the Youth Committee he started a summer youth conference. As chairman of the Sunday school and children's committee he encouraged Christians from five denominations to print a graded Sunday school curriculum which is still being used.

As managing editor of the church paper his writings influenced many. As district superintendent in Cairo he visited new groups and helped them to become self-supporting churches. As General Conference secretary he brought wise counsel to the conference. As delegate to the Free Methodist World Fellowship in Winona Lake he represented the Egypt General Conference in an outstanding way, along with his friend Abdu Fahmy.

In searching for the secrets of his unusual life, we must return to Upper Egypt to a town called Ghanayim. This town is noted all over Egypt for its killings and other crimes. But it is also famous for its great revivals in our church. It was to this town that the youthful Labeeb went with his pastor to attend weekend evangelistic services.

The account of a memorable service is better told by Labeeb himself as he wrote about his conversion: "On January 19, 1935, my pastor jumped up, shouting 'Hallelujah,' and I was too embarrassed to sit beside him. So I moved to another place, only to find myself beside someone who got on his knees and prayed, 'O Lord, cleanse me.' So I left him also and began searching for a quieter place.

"Pastor Black was preaching that day, with the help of the Holy Spirit, from the text, 'For our light affliction, which is but for a moment, worketh for us a far more exceeding and eternal weight of glory' (II Corinthians 4:17). He directed his remarks to sinners who did not have this glory, while tears rolled down his cheeks as he wept over sinners.

"The effect of the sermon was marvelous. The Holy Spirit was poured out on the meeting. There was shouting, crying, dancing, and tears — so much so that one could not distinguish between the joyous dancing of the believers and the crying of the seekers.

"I was greatly convicted. My heart was gripped, and I cried, seeking mercy and salvation. Before the end of the meeting, I sensed that the Lord had forgiven all my sins. My heart was made over, I had faith within my newborn heart, the Lord controlled my life, the joy of the Lord filled me, and the peace of God was with me. At that time I was nineteen years old."

This joyous faith continued to increase in the life of Labeeb Ateyah as he served in his various assignments.

After a trip to Assiut, where the Executive Committee planned the conference of 1970, he told several that he would not attend conference. He sensed he was going to be taken home soon by God.

He had been ill for a year or so, and at one time was very ill, but recovered and went about his work. He told his wife shortly before he died that God would not heal him this time as He had done in the past. He told her that God would help her and strengthen her to help the children.

His communion with God seemed to be such that he knew what was going to happen. Perhaps it was with him as it was with his mother who, just before she died, began to call out the names of the members of the village church in Salamone who had died before her. She seemed to be seeing them and greeting them after an absence from them.

Pastor Labeeb has also joined the company of believers from Salamone and from all over the world.

— Dateline: April, 1973

HONG KONG
SERVICE FROM A WHEELCHAIR
by Alton A. Gould

WHILE going among the wooden huts, a small window, perhaps a foot square, was opened by sliding back a board shutter. A face almost skeleton-thin, haggard, and white as death appeared. The long, uncut, uncombed mass of hair standing on end was enough to tell that this person had not been out of the hovel for a long time.

Making our way around a wooden hut, down a long unlighted dark, dirty hall we came to a small board bed. This was the only space this man could call home. No ventilation, no privacy, no one to care for him. A young man paralyzed from the waist down. How could he possibly live in such conditions?

The only money he had was what he could earn by lying on his back, putting tufts into toothbrushes with his bony, hawklike fingers. With this money he had to buy his rice and also hire someone to prepare his food. Depending upon neighbors with problems of their own too big to care for another!

The story of his gradual "uphill" climb is long. Over two years long! But Christ has worked a miracle in this man's life. No, he is not healed. That is, his earthly body is not healed, but yes, his soul is healed. The joy bells have been set ringing, and he has a home prepared for him. He has hope.

Later he told us that when we came to him he was planning to slash his wrists in order to end his unbearable life. He had no hope — no one to love or care for him.

Now he has hope, love, and that love is Christ Jesus. Christ is a very real presence in his life. Prayer has become like breathing to him. He asked God to heal him. God sent a wheelchair! No, the prayer wasn't answered in the way he expected, but it was answered. Praise His wonderful Name. We have told friends of this young man's need and God laid it on a doctor friend's heart in America to send him a canvas (oh so comfortable for that twisted, warped spine which had been lying on wooden boards), aluminum (so light for his weak arms to push anywhere himself) wheelchair.

No, the change wasn't sudden. It takes a long time for malice, hate, hopelessness to be replaced by the fruits of the Spirit. Each fruit was won by prayer. Faith had to be learned the hard way.

Hadn't he been turned out by his family because he was a cripple? How could he know these foreigners had anything real to offer?

He was ready to accept and believe and on his board bed to work for Jesus — not for the pay of money but for Jesus! Stamping and praying individually over tracts — thousands and thousands of them which are distributed by the workers — each one stamped with an invitation to attend Chapel. Bit by bit he grew.

The man inside grew to an adult Christian. A man who can do several jobs and care for himself. He baby-sits; he teaches school to several small children unable to pay the high fee to attend a regular school; but his regular job is using his little electric sewing machine to make cotton garments for a factory (this machine a gift from many friends). Truly he was raised from death unto life.

He is a constant daily testimony among all with whom he comes in contact of the saving, the satisfying, the real way of the gospel of life in Christ Jesus. His joy is to pay weekly visits to one of the hospitals nearby, visiting and telling others of this wonderful Christ.

— Dateline: January, 1959

HONG KONG

A Miracle Overcoat
by Alton A. Gould

It was a very cold day in February. One of our pastors called asking whether we had an overcoat for one of the members. This man had just managed to get a job as a night watchman after years of unemployment but didn't have proper clothes to keep himself warm. He needed an overcoat.

I promised to try to procure one for him, but after making some telephone calls, no overcoat!

That very afternoon the postman brought me a card advising me that a parcel had arrived and was awaiting collection at the office. When I took delivery of this parcel, I noted it was from Canada, and there was only one such parcel. Usually when the boat mail arrives, our letters, papers, and parcels are many, but in this one shipment there was only the one parcel.

Upon opening the parcel I found a beautiful brown overcoat (man's) inside with a wee note tucked inside:

"Dear Brother Gould, I am sending you this coat for some poor soul who is in need of one. I just bought it this morning thinking it was a good buy! The man was anxious to sell it, and I thought if I don't need it for myself, some poor soul would be glad for it at this time of year in needy Hong Kong. I am sending it to you as I feel that I must do this today, December 13th. I'm 83 years of age so do excuse the pencil writing."

One parcel arrived. I needed only an overcoat. That parcel contained only an overcoat and a man's at that! Here is a brother away over in Hong Kong and needing a coat, and another dear brother away up in Canada purchased the coat and mailed it. It took over five weeks to come, but it arrived the very day which this brother needed it in Hong Kong! "Before ye call, I will answer, saith the Lord."

— Dateline: December, 1963

INDIA

HIS NAME IS JOSEPH
by Gertrude Alcorn

I did not go to the hills this year and now am glad because I was here to help a man when he came inquiring about salvation.

One evening when I went to bed I was heavyhearted. I thought how often we had told the people about Jesus and yet they were so indifferent and would not accept Him. My heart was so burdened I could not sleep and I prayed, "Lord, there are some people in India who are hungry for Thee. Help us to find the hungry ones."

The very next day an intelligent-appearing man came to the bungalow. When I said to him, "Is there anything you want?" he replied, "I want to be a Christian." He was very much in earnest and showed me his English Bible and Hindi New Testament, the latter marked where he had studied it.

He told me his story. Ramchandra — as he then was called — was well educated first in the Benares Hindu College, then in a special school for Hindu priests. Walking one day in a garden in Kashmere he met an English padre (clergyman) who talked with him about salvation. This was a new idea to him and when the gentleman offered to give him an English Bible on condition that he would read it, the young man accepted the gift.

For sometime he read it secretly, since the

Hindu college forbade the reading of any but Hindu scriptures. After graduating he traveled with other young priests and several gurus (religious teachers), visiting various famous shrines. All the time he was far from satisfied. Yet proud, a Brahmin, what need had he of salvation?

But one night he had a vision. Before him was a dazzling light and a cross with the word "mukti" (salvation) above it. He told his guru of this and of his faith that Jesus was able to save. Alarmed, the guru telegraphed to the boy's father for instructions. He wired back to take him away where there were no Christians. The group of students and gurus started but one night, at a station about 30 miles from Yeotmal, he left the train while the others slept. Taking only a little with him he made his way on foot, first to Yeotmal and then to Darwha. He was weary and foot sore from walking so far in the very hottest weather. I saw the man was in earnest so invited him to abide with us for a while.

He knew his Bible better than our Christians and his influence among them was good. After a week he was baptized. Before the ceremony he removed the sacred thread which all Brahmin men wear and had the little tuft of hair on the back of his head cut off. He changed his name from Ramchandra — the name of a Hindu god — to Joseph. He is now in the Bible school in Yeotmal.

He has expressed a desire to go back to his home country, Nepal, and preach to his own people. He is asking us now to pray that he may receive the Holy Spirit. People who carry the gospel have not been permitted to go very far into Nepal yet.

— Dateline: November, 1941

INDIA

Two Annas and a Prayer
by Lois E. Kent

THAT year the garden of the Kline Sahib was unusually beautiful. Many times the weary missionaries wandered thither in the evening to rest tired bodies and relax taut nerves. Evening time seemed especially beautiful, with the sun low on the horizon, its lengthened rays shining softly through the leaves of the trees along the edge of the orange grove, and then the softened rays shining on the brilliant poinsettias turning their petals to velvet, and reflecting their warm hues over the whole garden. The tinkle of the bells on the bullock carts faded away gradually in the distance. The dust from the roadway seemed to sink tiredly to rest. The birds twittered their good-night messages, and the air seemed filled with calm and beauty. It was refreshing. It made one think of another garden of old, where One walked, and those who listened could hear His voice as He walked with them in the cool of the evening.

On that particular evening, a doctor paced wearily back and forth. Yes, the bewitching hour of the garden had arrived, but this time the doctor did not notice the beauty of the flowers, the softening rays of the sun, or the gradual quietening of the sounds around. He had reached one of those dark hours which inevitably come into the lives of all doctors, when they feel their human knowledge and strength has been insufficient and they must yield to a higher power.

Within the bungalow behind the garden was lying a missionary critically ill. Days previously an undiagnosed tropical fever had seized the young madamsahibah. No medicine would relieve it; nothing seemed to give help. Day after day the madamsahibah's fever would rise to record peaks and then ebb away for a while, leaving a thoroughly worn-out patient. What was causing it? What more could be done? Could the patient go through another day of it? Surely a critical stage had been reached. Even at that very moment the fever was raging at an unprecedented height. Thoughts of sad and dark import were running through the tired mind of the doctor. And what about prayer? Prayer had been made unceasingly ever since the beginning of the illness; everyone had been praying and was still praying, but day after day crept by, and still there was no abatement of the fever.

The doctor continued to pace to and fro. How could such a valuable life be lost? How could one allow such a beloved fellow missionary to slip away? But what more could be done? The nearest hospital was over a hundred miles away, and even then the moving of the patient would mean certain death. It was a dark hour in the garden of the Kline Sahib.

Then into the deep dark thoughts of the doctor penetrated a soft voice. "Dr. Missisahibah, Dr. Missisahibah." Finally she became aware of the gardener speaking to her. In his soft Indian language he asked "And how is Madamsahibah tonight?"

"Oh, Marley, she is very, very ill tonight. She

is not any better. We have done all we can, but she is worse tonight. You must pray, Marley; only God can help our Madamsahibah now and make her well."

"Dr. Missisahibah, we are praying, we are praying all the time. I pray all the time. I work, yes, but all the time I pray also, and I ask God please to make Madamsahibah well again. And Dr. Missisahibah, after much praying the Lord Jesus said to me, 'Do you really mean what you pray, and are you really in earnest that Madamsahibah be well again? If so, what will you give as thanksgiving to show that you really mean your prayer?' Dr. Missisahibah, I am a very poor man, as you well know. Already I give my tithe to the Lord Jesus, and that leaves me very little for my wife and children. So I said, 'Lord Jesus, I will give you one anna [two cents] if you will only make Madamsahibah well again.' Then the Lord Jesus said, 'You will give one anna for the life of Madamsahibah?' Then I said, 'Lord Jesus, I will even give two annas [four cents] for the life of the Madamsahibah.' And the Lord Jesus heard me and answered, 'Madamsahibah will be well again.' Oh, Dr. Missisahibah, I know Madamsahibah will be well again. Praise the Lord, I know she will."

Gradually the soft words crept into the weary mind of the doctor. What is this? Two annas, four cents, for the life of the missionary? She raised her eyes and looked at him. There he stood, a small dark figure in the gathering dusk of the garden. His watering cans stood on the ground beside him. His eyes, filled with tears, were lifted upward and his face shone with the love and glory of God. The doctormissisahibah knew, too. The Lord God had been walking in the garden of the Kline Sahib. He had spoken to a humble gardener, and the gardener had listened to Him.

From that evening the Kline Madamsahibah began to get well. The next day two annas were received as a special offering into the Lord's treasury.

— Dateline: April, 1944

INDIA

YOU'LL NEVER GET WATER THERE
by Rolland N. Davis

ONE of our semiretired preachers is living on one of the farms at Arjuna, some seven miles from Yeotmal. His home, built on the farm which he is buying from the Mission, is perhaps three hundred yards from the village and the nearest well. Regularly, he arose about four o'clock in the morning to go and carry his water for his home and young fruit trees before the morning rush from the village began.

To save carrying water so far and to be able to have a better garden at home, he decided to dig a well on the property he was buying. He borrowed some money from the Co-operative Society, arranged with the people to do the digging, and showed them where he wanted the well to be dug. "You'll never get water there," they remonstrated. So agreed the villagers.

"But I have prayed to my God about it and I believe He will give me water here."

"You may have prayed to your God, but we don't believe you can get water in that place," they insisted.

He prepared to dig. He gave a little feast to the diggers, and on the morning when they were to start to dig, he gathered the men and women together on the spot, opened his Bible, and read some verses. Then he prayed that God would give them water. After that, they started to dig in the black field earth.

They had not gone down more than a few feet when they struck a very hard layer of rock. The people were quite discouraged. The thought came to the preacher, *Well, perhaps I have made a mistake and should not have started here.* As he thought and prayed, however, he felt that they should dig on. For fifteen days, they sweat and labored, slowly making their way down through the hard rock.

Then they struck softer rock again, and the work began to go faster. When they were nearly twelve feet down, the soft rock appeared damp. One day the husband had gone to Yeotmal, and when he came back rather late, his wife said, "They have struck water."

In the morning he went to see, and truly there was water. In the burning, hot, dry season, having dug down twelve feet, they had two feet of water. He has walled up the well with rock two feet thick. The rock they dug from the hill not far away. He should now have a good supply of water the year around.

The villagers are still wondering that God gave them water in a place where they said, "You'll never get water there."

— Dateline: September, 1946

INDIA

LOVE OVERCOMES
by Frank and Betty Kline

SOME of you will remember the story of the first Bible School visit to Taroda village in 1938. At that time some of the "outcaste" people there had just become Christians, and they had invited Frank and Mr. Timothy and some of the students to their village. That night they all had dinner together and the next morning they took their guests out to inspect the fields. As they passed the village well, Mr. Timothy and Frank looked in it to see the condition of the water. They then went on to see the farms, but as they were coming back to the village they were astonished to see many of the caste people coming out with sticks and stones to drive them away. The leader of the group was a high caste man named Jairam, the headman of the village. The Lord helped Frank to have wisdom for the situation, and he asked Jairam if they might come to his house for tea. He was too surprised to refuse, so he took them to his house, and thus a riot was averted.

The trouble, however, did not stop there. The caste people thought that the well had been polluted because a foreigner had touched it, so for months they persecuted the Christian people of the village and would not allow them to draw water from the common well. Even when the Government declared the well open to all castes, they defiled the well many times, and left it to the Christians, while they themselves drew water from a private well. During all this trouble the Christians held firm and did not retaliate, but showed the love of Christ.

After some time a fine Christian pastor, John, went to live in the village, and his faithful life and witness began to have an effect on the caste people. Even Jairam, the headman, became his friend, even though he would not be friendly with the village Christians yet. Then in 1946, Marcus, the leader of the Christian group in Taroda, was greatly blessed at camp meeting, and the Lord enabled him to go back home and bring about a reconciliation between Jairam and the Christians.

In 1947 the Bible School on Wheels went back there with the Roots and evangelist Moses David for a revival meeting. At that time Jairam attended all the prayer meetings and preaching services, and would sometimes sit and weep silently, but he still made no public confession. When the team went on to the next village, however, he followed them there, openly repented, gave his testimony, and was baptized. Love had overcome!

Soon after it was discovered that Jairam was a leper. Arrangements were made for him to enter a Christian Home for lepers in a neighboring mission. There, because of his testimony that the Lord can save high caste people as well as outcastes, two of the Hindu lepers were saved.

Now Jairam has been healed of his leprosy through the love of Christ and the loving ministry of His servants, and is back in Taroda again. He is carrying on the way of love by serving under the Government as an instructor for adult illiterates in his village. Love does overcome!

— Dateline: September, 1949

INDIA
. . . FOR THE HUNGRY
by Nellie M. Jones

HAVE you ever been hungry? *Really* hungry? For more than a few hours at a time? Never knowing what it is to have hunger fully satisfied? Some people in this world *do* know; and this is the story of what one man did about it.

India is the locale — some of the Indians of Maharashtra State in Central India are the ones who were hungry — and missionary Rolland Davis and the lowly soybean vie for position of hero.

Hunger was a centuries-old problem; and the hungry lacked the energy and initiative to seek practical solutions. Back in 1953 Mr. Davis, convinced that India was overlooking an inexpensive and easy way to help the economy, began experimenting with growing soybeans in Central India — this under the direction of Dr. Cartter of the University of Illinois. Dr. Cartter sent out 23 varieties of the bean which he had selected as probably the most suited to that part of India.

"At first there was little interest in this crop," wrote Dr. Davis. But as he persisted through the next eleven years, planting altogether 59 varieties, he found four which proved to be "very good producers" for the area, with six others moderately good. "It has proven to be one of the most dependable crops in the district," he reports. Now the government has taken up the matter, and is urging the farmers to raise soybeans. Progressive farmers are also becoming interested and a soybean association has been organized. It includes leading governmental agricultural officers, other government officers, two newspaper men, a lawyer, and some progressive landlords of the district. A newspaper man said, "Now the raising of soybeans is going to increase rapidly."

And why is the soybean so valuable? Here are a few of the people who use it: operators of flour mills, drug researchers, makers of antibiotics, vegetable oil manufactures, makers of paint, producers of feed for animals and poultry.

In the category of food for human beings, the flour of the bean is used in preparing bread, noodles, soups, sweets, ice cream powders, breakfast foods, and as an extender of meat products. The protein content is higher than rice, wheat flour, and several other grains used in India. Since the average Indian diet is deficient in proteins, vegetable oils and calories, soybeans are of real value in making up these deficiencies. In addition, the beans produce more usable material per area than most other crops.

The oil and its other by-products are used widely in manufacturing paints, plastics, linoleum, artifical rubber, soap, glue, lubricating greases, fertilizers, disinfectants, oilcloth, printing inks, waterproofing for cement, textiles, and other articles. Important industries in India had been importing soybean oil and its products because they could not obtain them locally.

Not only does this wonderful bean provide food for the family and cash for the farmer when sold, but it also provides feed for any stock he may have. It enriches his soil, instead of depleting it. It is low in carbohydrates, so is excellent for those suffering from diabetes. It is high in vitamins. Its protein value is great — one pound of soybean flour is equivalent in protein to two and one-half pounds of beef, or 54 eggs, or nearly eight quarts of whole milk. In India one pound of the flour would cost approximately as much as one-quarter of a pound of meat.

All these facts Mr. Davis gathered and set forth. However, another impediment remained — the people did not like the taste of soybeans. So Mr. Davis has also gathered extensive information as to the use of this food in such a way that it will be acceptable — even to stating that in "wheat bread and other bakery products two or three parts of the usual flour and one part of soybean flour give a tasty product."

Persistence and faith and prayer have paid off. The soybean association "kindly garlanded myself as the outgoing president," wrote Mr. Davis; and he was thrilled to hear the different persons present tell how many acres they were going to plant in soybeans for the coming year. Thus Mr. Davis has been used of the Lord to help not only Indians at large in his area, but also those of the India Free Methodist Church, to see how they can do something about hunger, poor nutrition, poverty. Through the common soybean he has shown how they can become stronger physically and economically. With improved economy the Christians will find it possible to better support their own church.

Central India in general and the Free Methodist Indians in particular will long remain indebted to the Rev. Rolland N. Davis.

— Dateline: March, 1965

JAPAN

REV. T. KAWABE'S BIRTHDAY
by Ruth Mylander

O N the afternoon of April 14, according to a Japanese custom, and at the invitation of Brother Kawabe's son, Mitsu, we assembled at the big Nippon-Bashi church to celebrate the seventy-seventh birthday of this pioneer missionary to Japan.

Several representing the preachers, the church and so forth brought messages of tribute and praise, but gratitude and esteem were shown more by the large assembled audience, men and women, young and old, preachers and laymen, from far and near.

The greater part of the meeting was given over to Brother Kawabe and his testimony. He said that to tell of his life of seventy-seven years could not be done in one or two days, so he would speak briefly on only some parts. His remarks were given under four headings:

First, he spoke of the unsaved period of his life, twenty-three years. Born in a well-to-do home, he had no special trials or difficulties. His parents were earnest Buddhists who carefully taught him that religion, but it brought him no satisfaction or peace. He then studied Confucianism with the same results but with increased suffering. So he decided that money must be the source of peace. Therefore he went to America to make money, worked honestly and diligently and succeeded quite well.

Secondly, he spoke of the period of fifty-four years, after he became a Christian. God had mercy upon him a long time and then graciously opened his eyes blinded by money. In November, 1887, he was born again. At last he found true peace. It had not always been sunshine; there had been clouds and rain as well, but the joy and satisfaction remained unchanged.

Thirdly, he spoke of his fifty-two years as an evangelist. Two years after his conversion in a revival meeting in San Francisco he was sanctified and his life completely changed. God was made first in his life. Calamity, trouble, sickness and everything were taken to God in prayer. Previously he had gone to the doctor but since he was saved he has not paid one cent to a doctor except to a dentist once. When preaching at ten churches in Tokyo at one time he got a boil on his face. The lady where he was staying had had experience as a nurse and she said it was a malignant carbuncle and he ought to see a doctor, but later it came to a head and when opened soon healed.

When in need of money he told God only and never once had gone into debt. When called to go to Japan he had only five cents in his pocket; still he started to prepare and then someone offered to pay his passage and all expenses. Once when two bags of rice had been delivered but there was no money to pay for them, his companion asked what he should do. Brother Kawabe replied, "We'll drink soup till money comes." He got married on two yen rather than go in debt for the things he wanted.

In the early days, when he had been accepted as a Free Methodist missionary he had a small Bible school for which he received 150 yen per month from America. Without any previous notice this allowance was suddenly cut off. That was a hard experience but he told no one and did not go into debt. During those fifty-two years there had been many trials and difficulties but also great joy and thanksgiving continuously.

Fourthly, he mentioned his forty-five years of married life. When he began as an evangelist, thinking he could serve God better as a single man, he decided not to marry, but friends persuaded him that that was a mistake. He turned to his wife saying, "When I married this white-haired lady beside me, she was young and had beautiful black hair. I was a hot-tempered youth, and she not so gentle. We were like a tiger and lion living together!

Had I not been saved I might have beaten to death one or two wives, but in all these 45 years we have not had one family quarrel. She has been a great help, blessing and comfort to me. God has given us two children who are following in our steps. Many, many thanks to you, one and all."

— Dateline: November, 1940

JAPAN

STREPTOMYCIN HAVE I NONE
by Edward C. John

THREE weeks ago one of the young men who attends our seminary came to see me. Word had just come from his cousin telling him that his only son, a boy of six, was dying with pleurisy, and if he could get some Streptomycin for him, it might save his life. Would the missionary, please, get it for him? All the time he was making his appeal, the tears were freely running down his cheeks. He said, "My cousin is a widow and this is her only child, and she is not a Christian. Maybe if you can help her, she may become a Christian."

What would you do? This is one of the drugs that we are not allowed to bring into Japan. As I listened to his story, my heart went out in sympathy to him, but I felt so helpless that I breathed a prayer to God for guidance. Like a flash the words of the Great Commission came vividly, especially the promise. Matthew 28:19-20, "Go ye therefore . . . : and lo, I am with you alway, even unto the end of the world." Smiling through my tears I said, "I am sorry I do not have any Streptomycin, and I can not get it for we are not allowed to have it, but I know One greater than the drug and He loves us and will help. I will call my wife and Miss Fensome and we will pray, laying our hands on you for the little boy, asking

The Lord Jesus to make him well. He will not fail us for He is The Great Physician."

The young man's faith was inspired and he said, "I know that Jesus can make him well."

My wife, Miss Fensome, and I knelt down and prayed, laying our hands on the young man. We told Jesus how helpless we were, but that we were depending on Him and expecting and believing that He would heal the little lad at that very moment. What a blessed moment as the assurance came to our hearts.

The young man wrote to his cousin, and told her the time that we had prayed, and how God had given us the assurance that her son was healed. He exhorted her to give her heart to Jesus. The other day at seven-thirty in the morning, he was back to give me the news. He had a letter from his cousin saying that at the very hour we had prayed, her son was instantly healed and they had not understood it until his letter of explanation came. She is so grateful she wants to become a Christian. Smiling through tears of joy he said, "My faith has been greatly strengthened. Oh! How I love Jesus. He is wonderful.

—Dateline: September, 1949

JAPAN

Farmer Missionaries
by Alice Fensome

WIDE fields stretch away to distant California mountains. Hot sun beats down on hundreds of sweating farm laborers bent over short-handled hoes. The rise and fall of the hoes is accompanied by the rise and fall of Japanese voices.

Who are these Japanese? They are called "Tanno" — a word formed by combining two characters which mean "short-term farm laborer." In 1956, under the co-sponsorship of the United States and Japanese governments, a plan was formulated which allowed young farmers from Japan to study agricultural methods while working in California harvest fields. Since the initiation of this joint program 3,600 farm workers, from eighteen to thirty-five years of age, have come to the States, and 1,215 are still here.

When the Tanno reaches California he lives in barracks in his assigned area. He must provide his own food and do his own housekeeping and laundry. His work in the fields lasts from eight to ten hours. The barren living quarters and unaccustomed, monotonous work do not coincide with the dreams he had while in Japan. Sometimes his frustration leads to deep discontent.

One day in 1958, seventy-five-year-old Rev. Y. Shigekawa, pastor emeritus in the Pacific Coast Japanese Conference, received a letter from a Tanno. The young farmer bluntly expressed his discontent with his life in America and his particular hatred of the drinking water in the area where he worked. The next day the Rev. Mr. Shigekawa, armed with his Bible and a big jug of water, made a one hundred mile trip to meet the young farmer. That was the beginning of the Tanno Evangelistic Project which is now carried on by the Pacific Coast Japanese Conference. Since that day in 1958 over seventy young farmers have accepted Christ as Saviour, and over one hundred are still seeking.

In Japan one of the most difficult groups to reach with the gospel is the farmer. Up at sunrise and working until he can no longer see, he is too tired to bathe, change clothes and attend an evening service. Ultra-conservative, he does not desire change in habits of religion. Missionary effort in Japan has been largely urban, and rural areas are still practically untouched. A recent *Japan Harvest* survey reveals that "sixty percent of Japan's villages are without even the minimum witness of a Bible class or visiting preacher." The majority of the Tanno now working in California had never seen a church nor a Bible, nor heard the name of Christ in Japan.

Realizing the spiritual needs of the Tanno and the *latent potential for the evangelization of rural Japan through them,* the Pacific Coast Japanese Conference officially adopted Tanno Evangelism as their missionary project in 1963. At the annual conference in July, 1964, the Rev. Mr. Nobuo Ichihara was appointed as full-time missionary to the 1,200 young farmers in California. A Bible correspondence course was secured from a broadcasting company in Japan so that follow-up work can be done by the radio group when the farmer returns to his homeland. The laymen of the conference entered the picture in February, 1964, when the Tanno Evangelism Movement was organized at Glendale, California. The group meets for prayer and discussion of the Tanno problems. They collect funds for literature. Once a month they mimeograph a news sheet. The WMSers have become "California mothers" to the young farm workers.

Last Christmas nine young men were baptized at Indio where the Rev. and Mrs. Shigekawa still work among the Tanno. One, Yoshio Kasamoto, feels called to Brazil to work among Japanese immigrants. When he returns to Japan he must finish high school. He then hopes to attend the Free Methodist college in Osaka.

Mr. Harada, saved through the ministry of the Shigekawas in Indio, returned to Japan in the fall of 1962. Before returning to his village he purchased 50,000 yen ($140) worth of Sunday school supplies in Tokyo. Mr. Harada carries a deep burden for the salvation of the children of his village yet untouched by the gospel.

Another young man completed his three-year term in the States, returned to Japan, married, and this spring went to Paraguay. "He had such a wonderful testimony," states Mrs. Rowena (Kubo) Ichihara, "and he writes that he will build a good foundation in Paraguay to prepare the way for other immigrant Christians from Japan."

In the Anaheim area one of the first young men saved under the ministry of the Rev. Mr. Okamoto was Mr. Namba. In his last testimony before returning to Japan he said. "I am so happy to be a Christian. The first thing I shall do when I get home is to tell this happiness of Christ to my parents." Mr. Namba is the first Christian witness in his village. A recent letter tells of persecution.

Mr. Sugiyama, also of the Anaheim area, was saved last year through the death of a friend. Concerned for the salvation of his fellow-workers he has decided to dedicate his life to full-time Christian work. Writing to the Ichiaras of a service conducted by the Nisei (second generation Japanese) of the Los Angeles church he said, "I have very good news. Mr. Fukuma decided to accept Christ through the meeting last night. He used to say, 'I will never become a Christian even if I die.' He attended meetings a few times but said it was because of obligation. He said he regretted attending church the first time, but now has decided to become a Christian! How wonderful! He told me about his acceptance of Christ this morning as we were working together in the fields and my heart leaped with joy all day long. I cannot express this blessing of God. I just praise the Lord, hallelujah."

Testifying of this transformation in his own life Mr. Fukuma wrote, "I have been in America for a year. In the beginning I was under such a strain that I worked very hard. But the more I got acquainted with American life the more I became lazy and selfish and failed repeatedly. My heart was steeped in vice. I had no peace in my heart. But last night I came to realize that Christ Jesus can take away my sins. The testimonies of Mrs. Sagawa and Frank Sato were very meaningful to me. Their Christian faces are so shining and serene. I wonder if I, a melancholy person, can be like these Christians. I do not want to be a hypocritical Christian so please guide me."

— Dateline: January, 1965

MEXICO
AN EVENING'S REPORT FROM MEXICO
by B. H. Pearson

STEP over the Border with us tonight into that other world we call Mexico. You will not mind if I fail to tell you the name of the town. It really doesn't matter.

Soon we are in a district which goes by a fashionable name in the United States and speaks of the wealth of the aristocracy. The name has been borrowed in bitter irony for a region where strange, crooked lanes run every which way through the rows of huts whose walls have been formed of the same brown earth that makes the floors. As we approach, the place suddenly seems alive with dogs which rush from the doorways. Their wolfish forms are strangely frightening in the dark and well may we keep our guard. A man was brought down by them only recently and but a short time ago a girl was killed. Our guide flashes a light in their eyes to blind them and swings a piece of pipe that he has brought for protection. Soon we reach the rough mission building from which the gospel work is being carried on in this neighborhood. But let us listen to the worker this evening as he brings his report:

"The people here are very much blessed. Every morning they come and ask me, 'How is your heart today? Do you have peace? Are you happy?

Do you believe that God is going to give you new souls today?' If I cannot answer, 'Yes' then they pray for me. At the end of the day they come again and ask me, 'How many souls has God given you today? Have you had victory today?' They expect God to give us souls every day.

"The two girls who lived here as missionaries won their hearts. When they had to leave, the people were greatly saddened. When it seemed that the girls could not return, they went to prayer and asked God to make workers out of them. Now they are going out every day and trying to win their friends for Christ. They say, 'God took our workers, but he made us all workers and missionaries.'

"One night a man came into the service rather hurriedly. He was an old man converted only three days before on Sunday, and then he had testified with great joy on Monday. This was Tuesday night. He arose as soon as he could and said, 'My wife is sick tonight, but I told her I had to come over here, and so I arranged to get away for a little while. I must ask you, why is it that when I was so happy on Sunday when God saved me and so joyful all day yesterday that today I have lost my joy, there is no more joy in my heart? I have come here for you to tell me why the joy has gone out of my heart and why I am sad tonight.' Yes, he wanted to have a recipe right away so he could get his joy back.

"I told him, 'God's Word says "Is any among you sad, let him pray." What you need to do is pray, and we will pray with you.' So we dropped to our knees and had a wonderful prayer service. When we arose this old man was wiping the tears away from his face. 'How is your heart?' they asked him. 'It is all right now,' he answered. 'I have my joy back now.' And so he went on back to his sick wife.

"Sister _____'s son was absent from home, off in the deepest wickedness and sin. We prayed and the Lord answered and sent her son back home. But he became devil-possessed. He commanded at once that there be no more prayer meetings there. His mother told us, 'We cannot have more prayer meetings here.'

"The brethren went to visit him, but the young man was very serious. He could not talk. He was dumb. Something seemed to have control of him and he could not speak. As the men knelt to pray for him, something indicated to Brother R_____ that he should put his hands upon this wicked young man and invoke the name of the Lord, pleading for the evil spirit to leave him. After the prayer his mother asked him, 'J_____, how do you feel?' 'Now, I feel better,' he answered and after this he could talk. 'Pray for me that I may get another job,' he requested, for he is a barkeeper in a saloon and a member of the barkeeper's syndicate. He cannot leave, it would seem, nor can he find other work. But he must.

"His mother was baptized. The brethren said that she had idols in the house. (They meant the saints which are worshiped). I went and talked to her about the images which she had up in the niche in the house. She said, 'Oh, those dolls, they have ears but they don't hear, and eyes but they don't see,' and I thought, Where did she learn Scripture? 'What shall I do with them?' 'Break them up,' I said. 'I will break them up for you.'

"Her little boy came in then. 'Who put that idol down there?' he asked. 'What are you going to do with it? Going to bury it?' But the mother gave it to me. They also gave me a trunk of books of the Mass and Catholic prayers and the blessed palms from which to make sacred crosses.

"There was another Sister S_____ converted. We went to visit her. 'I cannot pray,' she said. 'Pray to God in the name of Jesus,' we told her. "I cannot," she answered. 'Then there is something that is hindering.'

"Brother R_____ said, 'You went with the spiritualists before and this little table with three legs over here in the corner which answers your questions — there is the trouble. What are you going to do with the table?' 'Burn it,' she answered.

"I reached up for it. 'Not tonight,' she protested. 'No, now!' I answered, and told the child to bring me the can of coal oil. I broke the table up and set fire to it. She was very happy about it. The man who was living with her came. He was very angry. 'But I bought it with my own money' she said, 'and this table was damning my soul.' The man was so angry that he left her. She has found work to help her sustain herself, but she greatly needs our prayers."

He continued, "J_____ V_____ went to Mexico with an automobile and money he received through compensation for a child burned to death in the United States. He started a saloon. Things went from bad to worse. He became poverty stricken. One day he came to us, 'Now I am ready to serve God,' he said. 'For I read in the Bible that one must leave wife and son and daughter for the sake of the Gospel. And I have left them.' He told us what had happened when we asked him. An argument had arisen. His wife had hit him with the rolling-pin with which she was making tortillas. That decided him to become a Christian! 'No,' said one of the brothers, 'you cannot get right with God until you get right with your wife.'

"We went to her to find out about it. 'Did you have a fight?' 'Why, he hit me,' she said. 'And you?' 'No, nothing.' 'Nothing?' 'Well, I hit him, and I had a rolling-pin in my hand,' she admitted.

At two o'clock that afternoon we had an evangelistic service and this man was saved and then reconciled with his wife. Now he has work.

"The other day Mrs. R_____ said, 'Brother, it would be well for you to visit a lady who is dying. She seems to be demon-possessed, for she is cursing and swearing.' She was 28 years of age but looked 55. She had gone to spiritualist meetings. Since then she had been deaf. I wrote a paper for her, 'Do you want to be healed?' She nodded her head. 'Mr. A_____ said, "No, ask her if she wishes to be saved." I wrote, 'Do you believe that Jesus Christ could save you?' She nodded. 'Do you wish that we pray to the Lord for you?' She nodded yes again.

"When we got up from our knees I wrote, 'Be of good cheer, daughter, thy sins are forgiven thee.' Then she spoke for the first time — 'Oh, what a great blessing you have been to me, what a help you have been. Keep on praying for me.' Soon she died."

The lights which had been shining through chinks in the wall of the nearby houses are now out. The dogs are quiet. The only sound is a guitar at some distance and the voices of two drunk men singing. As you look out into the darkness of that colony and think of what God is doing there, you need not ask yourself do missions in Mexico pay?

— Dateline: May, 1939

MEXICO
VICTOR
by Burleigh Willard

A victory celebration was in full swing. At the place of honor, enjoying it to the full, was Jose Aranda. Known in the ring as the Yellow Bear (El Oso Amarillo) he had just won the boxing championship of the state of Coahuila, Mexico. Drinks flowed freely, and Jose was more than a little tipsy when he reached home.

The days that followed were filled with more training and fights, but somehow the glamor was fading. Jose found himself drunk more and more. If he won a fight his friends treated him to drinks, and if he lost they tried to console him with alcohol. He had already begun to train his sons to be fighters, and both of them had experience in the ring as Yellow Bear II and Yellow Bear III. But Jose did not want his sons to become drunkards and he clearly saw where his career was leading him, for now he would drink for days at a time. Finally he quit the ring altogether and discouraged his sons from fighting.

About this time his younger son Victor, Yellow Bear III, had an interesting conversation with one of his friends. The friend had been away to school and painted an attractive picture of his school, his friends and the chance of an education. He scarcely mentioned that the school was a Protestant Bible school because he realized Victor knew very little about the gospel. He thought maybe Victor would be saved if he came to Nogales Bible School.

Adventure attracted Victor and he decided to go away to school with his friend. With two other companions he began the 1,500-mile trip across the Sierra Madre mountains to the city of Guadalajara, then up the scenic west coast of Mexico to Nogales, Arizona.

The school officials were not expecting him nor his two companions, Juan Rodriguez and Pedro Wong — a half Chinese boy — as they had not been properly recommended nor formally accepted as students. But it is hard to turn down a boy who has sold his school books to get enough money to travel 1,500 miles to school. So a way was found to include the adventurers.

Victor did not have the documents necessary to get a student passport so he had to stay for some time on the Mexican side of the international boundary with our pastor in Nogales, Sonora. The pastor, himself a young man, was favorably impressed with the boy. During the waiting time a Youth for Christ rally was held in the Free Methodist Church where Victor was staying. The preacher for the evening was none other than the Rev. Ramon Quintanar, Dean of Men at Nogales Bible School. When the invitation was given, Victor humbly knelt at the altar for prayer. This was the beginning of a new experience that was to grow into a deep and delightful dedication to God.

Victor was not accustomed to studying and it was sometimes hard to find the assignment in Hebrews or II Kings because he had never read a Bible before, but he applied himself. His quiet sincerity made him a favorite with his companions and his teachers.

His new-found joy was too good to keep and he began at once to write to his parents about it. Our pastor in a nearby town was informed about the family. Victor made sure the conference evangelist visited them when he was in that part of Mexico. The family was kind and open to the gospel because of Victor's testimony. In his first visit home the change in his life was so apparent that it had a telling effect.

In the summer of 1963 a missionary couple held a week of special meetings in Victor's hometown. One Sunday night preceding the service Mrs. Missionary used the feltogram and told the story of the prodigal son to the children. At the close she said, "I am inviting all of you who wish to accept Christ as your Saviour to indicate it by rising from your seat and coming forward." The first to rise was the former boxing champion. Unbelieving, his family saw his tears and heard his prayer of repentance. That night Jose Aranda gave his heart to the Lord. Only once since, and that soon after his conversion, did he come home drunk. He had been persuaded by his old cronies to take a drink and the inevitable happened. He arrived home so ashamed of his weakness, that he prayed earnestly for divine help and since that day has had a wonderful testimony of deliverance. Then the mother and an older sister were saved. Later Victor visited his home again and was able to lead his older brother, Yellow Bear II, to the Lord and save him from a divorce.

The Aranda family are now all saved — parents, three daughters, and two sons — as well as the husband of one of the daughters and the brother and sister-in-law of Jose Aranda. They have offered part of their lots for a church building. The Missionary Board is sponsoring an evangelistic team made up of two of Victor's schoolmates. They are holding services in the Aranda home and hope to soon organize a church there.

As for Victor, some months before his graduation when the director of Nogales Bible School asked him what his plans for the future were, he said quietly, as if he thought everyone should have known, that he intended to preach the gospel. And he is doing just that. He graduated in June, 1964, and is now serving as a pastor.

— Dateline: April, 1965

MOZAMBIQUE
Moonshine in Africa
by Victor W. Macy

"The revenue officers are coming! They've smashed our neighbor's still — there they come through the bush; grab the pipe, grab the jug, run, run!" Words to this effect are what you might hear if you were a little field mouse out in a clump of bushes where the heathen were illegally making beer on mission property — that is, if you were a field mouse who could interpret from Sheetswa or Sheechopi into English.

The natives distill "beer" from most anything — pineapples, oranges, corn, and especially the fruit of the cashew tree from whence we get those delicious cashew nuts. The "still" is a crude but effective affair consisting of a large clay pot on top of which is plastered upside down a smaller pot with a hole in one side. Beside this arrangement there is placed a bark trough, the height of this hole, which contains a pipe running the length of it. This pipe enters the clay pot at one end of the trough and extends out over a jug at the other end. Pipes are most essential and therefore the most valuable part of the equipment for they are the only part which cannot be native made. One sees all kinds and sizes and shapes — even old gun barrels. Some natives make a handsome sum going about the country selling these pipes which, though but three feet long, sell for around three dollars each.

When the proper time comes, the women, who are the beer makers, are sent out to pick up the fruit and bring it to the scene of the operations where it is stored in numerous pots to ferment. At the proper time the big pot of the apparatus is filled and a fire built under it; as the alcoholic steam rises it is caught by the upside-down pot and conducted through the pipe which is now submerged in water in the trough. Thus cooled, it is condensed and runs out of the other end into the jug as pure and powerful alcohol. A twig is usually found stuck in the end of the pipe, directed down through the mouth of the jug to conduct the trickle and keep the wind from blowing it away. Now from the jug you can imagine for yourselves where the alcohol goes and what it does!

Concerning the "revenue officers," or better, the demolishing officers. As such, our first experience was with Brother Arskey, and at that occasion we learned the technique — to break everything possible, to throw out all things "throw-outable" (this doesn't mean the operators; they've already taken to their heels to tell their neighbors to hide their pipes) and to carry home the pipes.

Well, with this lesson learned and our teacher gone for the summer, Susan and I started out alone, for though the Christians are glad to see us "kill" the stills they are afraid to go along; vengeance consists of perhaps a beating or a ruined garden. We soon learned where to look for these hidden stills, a clump of bushes a short distance from the hut with perhaps a thread of smoke emerging, or perhaps some muffled voices to betray the spot. Once spotted, then is the time to make a dash for it and reach the pipe before the owners are off with it or hide it in the deep bush.

After we had added a fourth pipe to our collection that first afternoon and were watching the steaming, smoking remains of the last still, through the bush came the indignant owner of the previous still and lovely long pipe. Now this *was* a new experience. He began pleading for his pipe with tears in his eyes; seeing that this method didn't work, he tried another, planting himself in our path, not letting us pass and shouting, "Kill me, but don't take my pipe." Well, you know, a missionary who comes to preach the gospel to the heathen couldn't very well do that; he must have seen our point of view, for of a sudden he grabbed the pipe, but I had a hold of it too and had had experience in playing tug of war. Well, it turned out to be a tie, for he was a husky fellow and Susan wasn't interested in taking part in our little game.

By this time it was getting dark and we were a good three miles from home *via* bush, so we decided we'd better tell the Lord about it. Down on our knees we went, I still held to the pipe. I prayed — there was a pretty good congregation by this time — while Susan watched, for an old woman was sneaking around to grab one of the pipes which she was holding. At the end of the prayer everyone said "Amen" as lustily as a lot of saints at a camp meeting — but my friend still held to the pipe. However, the Lord must have whispered something in my ear for I finally suggested to Susan in Sheetswa that she take the keys and go back to the house, get the car and bring a few police along from town — while I held the pipe. But alas, after all of our tearing here and there through the bush, Sue had to admit in English that she didn't know the way home; nevertheless she started out. Before she had gone more than fifty feet my opponent said in good Sheetswa, "OK., you win," or something like that, and we continued on our way rejoicing, adding another pipe yet to our collection before we reached home.

— Dateline: December, 1950

MOZAMBIQUE
BIOSO
by Lela DeMille

I remember meeting Bioso the first Sunday we were at Massinga — an old lady with troubled eyes and reeking of tobacco. Sister Jacobs spoke to her about the Lord, asking her if her heart did not want to live. She replied that her heart wanted the Lord. Sister Jacobs exhorted her to leave all her sins and turn to Christ.

Shortly after this the Jacobs left and since that time I have watched the development of this soul. In the early stages of learning the language how I longed to be able to point the way to her. My heart longed to help her but my tongue could not frame the words. But there was One more interested than I and He knew "Xitswa." He was leading.

Soon we noticed the absence of demon ornaments and bracelets. She was regular in attendance Sunday after Sunday. She began coming forward to the altar. Each time an invitation was given she would come forward weeping and kneel before the King of kings. Last February in our revival it was thrilling and refreshing to see the soul hunger of this child of God. Through the dew of early morning she trudged day after day to the prayer service. Few of the others, except our little inner group, found time for this early service. But Bioso was there pleading in her childlike way, "O Lord Jesu, I do not know the proper form of prayer, I am just an old woman, I have no eyes to read a book, but my heart wants You."

In her testimony recently she said, "The people named me Bioso (one who drinks and dances) because I used to drink so much, but I am not Bioso any longer. I have a new name because I am a new person. I do not want the darkness of this forest, I want to be a follower of Jesu. Once I trusted in the blood of animals, but now I trust in Jesu alone."

She was too old to learn many of the songs and her mind, grown old in sin and degradation finds it hard to grasp the truth of the gospel. But her face lights up when she sings — to the tune of "Sweetest Note in Seraph Song":

There is no name on earth
There is no name in heaven,
Which is greater than the name of Jesus.

One day while visiting with her I told her I wanted to take her picture.

"Take my picture," she asked, "what is that?" So I showed her some pictures and explained that I wanted to send her "face" to her friends in America. After a time she said, "Senhora, some day let us all go to your home in America." I replied, "Mother Bioso, that is impossible but to that home that Jesus has gone to prepare for us who love Him, yes, we shall all go some day." Her face lighted up as she heard with joy of a place where we shall never hunger nor thirst again; where we shall never know heat or cold again. This means more to her who is accustomed to feeling the gnawings of hunger and burning thirst than it ever can mean to you dear friends at home.

The old heathen chief wanted Bioso to become one of his wives. She refused and incurred his wrath. He said, "Many troubles will come your way because you refuse me." True to his word he has caused her much trouble, but thus far she has overcome through Christ.

— Dateline: November, 1941

MOZAMBIQUE
DOWN TO THE SEA IN SHIPS
by Mae P. Armstrong

At early dawn of April 17 the *Zam Zam* was shelled by a German raider. The passengers and crew all escaped in lifeboats or otherwise. Some were in the open sea for a time, including Margaret Thompson and myself. We were picked up by the raider's crew and put aboard the raider itself. We were there about thirty hours, then transferred to a German merchant vessel acting as supply ship for the raider.

We were on board this boat nearly five weeks, virtually prisoners but considered in their own terms as "involuntary guests." At no time were we treated unkindly by them. We were crowded, of course. Food was limited as to quantity and variety. We were under guard all the time. There were eight days and nights (the last ones of the voyage) when we had to sleep in our clothes ready to put on our life belts and escape at any hour of the day or night should an alarm be sounded. This was while we were passing through the danger zone off Europe and near islands.

On May 20 we landed at St. Jean de Luz, France, not far from the Spanish border. We were taken from there to Biarritz, France, by buses commandeered by the Germans who were occupying France. Here four hotels were used for our quarters while waiting for release. First came the Consul from Bordeaux, France, who cabled names of those there to Washington, D.C. Later came representatives from the American Embassy to Spain. These started negotiations with German, Spanish, and Portuguese authorities relative to moving us out of France, across Spain and into Portugal. This took considerable time, as all such "red tape" affairs do. But meanwhile we were well cared for by German Red Cross, had luxurious rooms and the freedom of the city after the first two days. It was a beautiful place, a popular summer resort of the wealthy and of royalty in prewar days.

On May 31 we started out again on buses, were taken to the Spanish border, where we took the train. Two days and two nights of travel brought us to Lisbon yesterday morning (June 2) where we were met by buses and brought here to be quartered in three hotels while waiting further.

Yesterday a member of the American Legation stated that a cable had just come from Washington, D.C., in response to a cable they had sent informing that many missionaries in this group preferred to continue their journey to Africa if the State Department would permit. Their answer was that all were to return to U.S.A. So now it is a question of when rather than what.

I saved some of my personal effects, three suitcases, most of my dresses, a little underwear, one pair of shoes and slippers, housecoat, kimona, spring coat, raincoat, new sweater, blue felt hat, purse, New Testament and Psalms, folding umbrella, writing case, fountain pens, passport, all important papers, money — so fared better than many.

The hardest part of it all has been not being able to let you know how we were and relieve your anxiety. The prayer meetings, continued every day, always included as one of the big petitions that all our "home folks" might be kept in that "perfect peace" we were enjoying.

— Dateline: July, 1941

MOZAMBIQUE
THEIR NAME WAS LEGION
by Susan Blair Macy

As we sat in the shade of a great tree, hidden deep in the African bush, I heard this testimony from the lips of a newborn child of God:

"My sister and I were born into a heathen family. When I was about eight years old, we moved our kraal to a different district. My parents feared the evil spirits, and so one of the first things they did after moving was to call a witch doctor to build and dedicate a demon hut in our village. He came and built the hut, called the evil spirits and dedicated the hut to them. Then he said to my parents, "You must give one of your daughters to serve these spirits — to be their priestess." My parents chose me as I was the elder. Then, after dedicating me to the work, the witch doctor went away.

"From that time on I did nothing but live for those evil spirits. My hair was covered with red clay, the badge of my office, and I literally gave myself to the spirits. They liked me. I became possessed of them. They came at my call. My duties were as follows: Each morning I got up and sat out in the sunshine resting while one of the members of the family swept out the demon hut. I was not allowed to do any work because it was my duty to keep quiet and entirely undisturbed by any unpleasant daily duties, so that nothing would interrupt my daily communion with the evil spirits. Each morning after the hut was cleaned I would go in with a gift of food, greet the spirits and ask for their protection over our village. Every evening also I went in with food to thank them for their help that day and to bid them good night.

"If a member of the family planned a visit it was my duty to enter the hut with a gift, call up the spirits, enter into communion with them through a trance and ask their protection for the journey. If no assurance of protection was given, the proposed journey was abandoned. If, on the other hand protection was assured, the journey was undertaken. After the traveler returned I again entered the hut with a gift of thanks. All gifts taken into the hut belonged to me. I ate the food, and the gifts of money bought my clothes as well as the adornments which the evil spirits commanded me to wear. I always had plenty of money because of the young men going and returning from Johannesburg. Another great source of income was the sacrifice made in case of sickness. Babies were always sick and much money and food was given to the spirits in their behalf. I sold many charms. Some were bought as medicine, but most of them served simply as visible proof to the evil spirits that the parents feared them and had sacrificed money to appease them.

"I continued in this work until I was sixteen years old. I never had any difficulties with the evil spirits. Nothing hindered our fellowship. They were very well satisfied with me. But I was by now of marriageable age. A young man came and paid my parents a good sum for me and I became his wife. At first this meant no great change for me because he moved to our village so that I might carry on with my work. Nevertheless, we did have some family troubles. One night the spirits came to me and said that they were putting money under my mat because in the morning they wanted me to go and buy a certain type of bracelet to wear in serving them as well as a special piece of black cloth to wear under my blouse.

"In the morning when we wakened I looked under the mat and there was the money. My husband was very angry and declared that I had been given the money by some other man in the village. He said that I had been unfaithful to him. I told him how the evil spirits had come to me in the night, but he did not believe it and he threw the money out into the bush. But the next night the evil spirits came again ordering me to buy the bracelet and cloth, promising to leave the money under the mat. In the morning, sure enough, it was there again. My husband saw it and believed. That morning he went to the store with me to buy the bracelet and cloth.

"During the next few years two children were born to us. Life went on much as usual, until one day my husband came home after a long absence and announced that he had become a Christian and that he had decided to move to a Christian village. Of course that made things difficult for me, but as he had paid for me I had to follow him. The witch doctor was called, and he gave my job to my younger sister. Then we moved into a Christian village.

"On entering the village I did not confess that I was demon possessed and so from the beginning I was ill at ease among the Christians. Moreover I was unwell in body. The evil spirits began to torment me and to urge me to return home. 'But,' I would say, 'my sister is there in my place, go to her.' But they did not accept my sister. I belonged to them and they wanted only me. I was not surprised, therefore, when word came from home that my sister was unsuccessful as priestess of the demon hut. She could not contact the spirits. My parents begged me to come back. But for some reason I was not anxious to return.

"After a while I became pregnant. It seemed that I was always ill. The evil spirits tormented me night after night throwing me into convulsions. Then I began to realize that they were making my baby sick within me. I began to fear that they would kill my baby. But still I was afraid to tell the Christians that I was demon posessed, nor did my husband confess it. Then one day it came to me that if I would confess I might save the baby. That night the evil spirits told me I would be terribly ill by morning if I did not promise to go home. I did not agree, and the next morning I was so ill I couldn't leave my mat to hoe in the fields. I could not eat and thought I would die. I recovered, however, but the fright I received from this sickness kept me from confessing that I was possessed.

"Pretty soon our baby was born — a sickly little thing. 'Now, I thought, 'I will not be sick any more.' But the spirits did not leave me, and to my horror I found that they had entered my baby also. From time to time when the spirits were visiting me my baby would go into convulsions. They were trying to force me to go home by tormenting the baby. Then I knew that I must get help from the Christians if I wished to save the baby. But the fear of the evil spirits kept my mouth closed.

"Several months passed. Baby became weaker and weaker. I knew that he was dying. In desperation, unable to bear it any longer, I went to evening prayers in the church and told the people that I was demon possessed. I asked their help. Then I went home to the worst experience of my life. During the night the evil spirits came in great power filling me completely. I started to leap and shout, and I went to such an excess that the whole village awakened hearing my screams. The Christians said the very house was shaking. Seeing my condition they caught hold of me and pushed me down on the floor. Then with their hands upon me they prayed that the Lord Jesus would deliver me from the power of the demons. I became quiet immediately.

"From that time on Baby and I have been getting stronger and stronger. The evil spirits have never again taken possession of me. When I feel them approaching, I kneel and pray or run to my friend, the evangelist's wife, and we pray together. Then the spirits always leave without harming me. I am praying that my Saviour will help me to keep trusting Him so that I may never fall into the possession of the demons again. I thank Him for His love. I am much better in my heart and my body now, and my baby plays happily. God is very great!"

— Dateline: October, 1948

MOZAMBIQUE

WE HAVE WAITED A LONG TIME
by Florence Carter

ABOUT six o'clock in the morning, as planned, I started out in the Land Rover to move evangelist Alfredo Hassani and his family to a new area. At a Massinga district quarterly meeting he had volunteered to go to Xipanzana to start a new work.

Alfredo and his family were ready when I reached his village. We packed the car with household goods, sacks and sacks of grain, crates of chickens and a dog, plus the Hassanis and their five children.

We drove on the main road until we came to the turnoff by a little store and then started into the bush. Somehow we missed the second turnoff that would take us to Xipanzana. We traveled for miles until Alfredo began to doubt whether he knew the way. When we made inquiry we were told to go ahead until we came to a certain tree and that road would take us to our destination. So off we went again and drove for many more miles. Every tree looked like the last one to me but Alfredo said we still had not arrived. Finally we came to open country where two women were taking water from a shallow well. They said the road was closed. So back we went the dusty miles to the little store on the main road where we once again asked directions.

Once more we started on our journey, confident we would reach our destination. But about an hour later I realized that even the deep sand would not cause the car to pull as it was doing. It was a flat tire! And it was high noon with a blazing sun above and only a few scattered trees for miles around.

I found the tools but neither Alfredo nor I could budge the nuts on the rim. We poured water, kerosene, and even liquid soap over them but to no avail. The jack kept sinking lower and lower into the sand. Swarms of horseflies added to our miseries.

As we worked at the car many people passed by. Everyone was astonished to see a white woman with a dirty, grease-streaked face out there in the bush. Their questions as to my reason for being there opened the way for a gospel testimony. Two men tried to help us get the tire off but decided it was an impossibility. By promising one of the men money when he returned, we persuaded him to go back to the main road for help. He started out shortly after five o'clock.

It was about this time that Alfredo discovered seven chickens had died from the heat. We decided to cook the three large ones as that was all the food we had. Mrs. Hassani found water. The children built a fire and started to pick the chickens, throwing the feathers in the fire. When the chicken was done they served mine on a clean plate that they found somewhere in the baggage.

Darkness and mosquitoes were all around us by eight o'clock. We decided to have evening prayers and then try to sleep. It was beginning to get chilly so we needed blankets. After much lifting of crates, pushing of sacks and pulling of many articles, we finally got the Hassanis' trunk out from under the sacks of grain. In so doing we cracked the car window. I took a tire tube from the toolbox, inflated it a little and folding it for a pillow, curled up on the car seat.

At midnight the barking of a dog aroused me, and I heard voices. Alfredo came to the car and said that the man we had sent to the little store on the main road had come back. With him was a second man carrying pliers and a pipe wrench. By two o'clock in the morning the tire was fixed. After a fourteen-hour delay we could once more begin to move. And just in time, for the rain began to fall.

We took a moment to praise the Lord and then were on our way. We could scarcely see the road. Sometimes there was only the parting of the tall grass to indicate where it might be. The sand was so deep I had to use four-wheel drive. I knew there were dangerous thorns and stumps out there in the darkness. I also knew this was snake, leopard, and elephant country. But I also knew the Lord was very near. As I intently watched the road and prayed I remembered that it was prayer meeting night in my home church.

Just as day was breaking we entered the little village where the Hassanis were to live until they could build their own house and start their own garden. The village headman was not there so Alfredo walked across the fields to another village. There the chief offered the use of a hut to store their goods so we drove over.

It seemed that time had passed that little village by. The sole occupants were old Chief Tawuzeni and his wife. Dressed in a tattered shirt-like upper garment and trousers of skin the chief came to greet us. His wife huddled in the background, amazed at the sight of a white woman. The chief's six-inch beard was tied with a rope from his chin downward. When he sat down by the fire he started to roll something in his hands. It took the form of a cigar. He didn't light it at once but stuck it in the large hole in the lobe of his ear. His wife brought him a bowl of food which he stirred with a wooden spoon before eating. Then she brought us some boiled water and I made instant coffee. I gave some to Alfredo and his wife. They put it into their coconut shells and drank it as they unpacked the car. That was our breakfast.

I asked the chief if he knew why Alfredo was moving to the village. He said he did and that he was very pleased that they were to learn about a Saviour. He said that both he and his wife wished to learn and that hundreds of people in the surrounding area were waiting to hear.

By seven o'clock everything had been taken from the car and stored in the hut. Alfredo and I prepared to return to his father's village for the rest of the household goods including the necessary cooking pots and bowls. Mrs. Hassani and the children were to stay in Xipanzana. Before leaving we had prayer together and the old chief looked so happy. He seemed to realize something new and wonderful was about to come into his life.

As we went back over the road we had traveled during the night and I saw the dozens and dozens of tree stumps, I wondered how I had ever avoided them in the dark. I am so thankful for prayer meetings!

After an hour of driving we overtook a man on a bicycle. We asked him to ride and he put his bicycle in the back of the Land Rover. He proved to be another Alfredo, and another evangelist. During the course of our conversation we learned that we were on the very same road that pioneer missionary J. W. Haley had traveled on foot and donkey as he explored the country forty years ago! Forty years of waiting for the gospel! Forty years with no message of a Saviour! But at long last an evangelist had come to Xipanzana!

(Six months later.) Fifteen people are now worshiping in Alfredo's village. Twenty-five attended the evening service in chief Tawuzeni's village. He is so happy that someone has come to teach him about Jesus. The waiting time has been so long.

— Dateline: February, 1965

PARAGUAY

Donya Leona
by Lucy Huston

THE first time I saw Donya Leona she was holding a hymnbook. A slight woman with faded head scarf and long cotton dress, she sat in front of me in the modest little church. Her high collar and long sleeves helped to almost completely cover her.

When we stood to sing, she held the book open and I saw her hands. They were small hands — small, but tough-skinned. Her fingernails were worn down to the fingertips. When she turned the pages of the book, I noticed that the backs of her hands were deeply wrinkled.

When the minister announced the scripture reading, Donya Leona turned to get her Bible. Lovingly, caressingly, she held it a moment, then turned quickly to the Psalms.

She stood erect. For three-quarters of a century Donya Leona had balanced burdens on her head. Carrying heavy cans of water, or baskets of bananas or chickens, or sometimes only a watermelon on her head helped to form her stiff posture. She bent her head to read, but her back remained straight as a papaya tree. The posture depicted a characteristic trait of her countrymen — a proud people. Her Indian and Spanish heritage gave her this pride — pride in that origin and pride in her soil.

Later, during the sermon, she leaned toward a tired-looking mother sitting beside her and took the sleeping child from the mother's arms. She cuddled the child and then wiped the perspiration from its head. I could see only her hands — all wrinkled, gentle.

At the end of the service Donya Leona turned to greet me. A toothless smile lit up her brown, wrinkled face. Her dark eyes twinkled, revealing a sense of humor unusual in a Paraguayan woman of her age. "Ba ai sha pa," she greeted me as she extended her hand to shake mine. Not ashamed that she spoke very little Spanish, she was proud of her native Guarani.

The next afternoon I went to visit Donya

Leona. She was in the yard, squatting before a three-legged iron pot, with a machete in her hand. She swung the long, heavy-bladed knife to chop a dead branch into shorter pieces for her fire. This little woman with the gentle, caressing hands showed strength and determination as she easily and quickly finished the chopping before turning to answer my clap at the gate.

During the course of our conversation I learned that Donya Leona was also a woman of faith and courage. She told me, "For fifty years my relatives have persecuted me because of my religion. When I became a Christian my husband and daughter left me. Then, when my son died, everybody said that it was because the witch doctor had put a curse on me. I had to move to the city to make a living. It is here in the city that I made a new life for myself. Fifty years ago very few of my people were Christians. But through the years I have seen many of them find the same peace that I have."

Lifting a Bible off the table, she quietly asked me to read for her the twenty-third Psalm.

— Dateline: April, 1971

PARAGUAY

THANKSGIVING
by Minoru Tsukamoto

It was about ten years ago when I met here in Paraguay a missionary by the name of Nahum Perkins. I was introduced to him by the

Rev. Ernest Huston who told me that Mr. Perkins would be helping our work for a while. I do not remember how long he worked with us, but I do remember that I interpreted his messages into Japanese in many different services. Some years after my happy experience with him I learned that he had gone home to be with the Lord.

A couple of weeks ago I met a Japanese woman on the dusty streets of Encarnacion. In our conversation my ears caught the name of "Nahamu Paakin Sensei" (Teacher Nahum Perkins). She reminded me of the visit of the missionary in her home in a jungle area ten years ago. You can imagine how my heart jumped up when I heard the familiar name. Nahum presented a Bible to the family as a reminder of him and his visit there. Ten years have passed since that little event in that home. And today — yes — after ten years, that woman was coming to see me to tell me that she and her whole family wanted to accept Christ and be baptized.

I took the visiting eight-member Nisei evangelistic team from the Nikkei Conference of Brazil to the home of that Japanese woman in the colony. Mr. and Mrs. Tanii and their parents were ready for accepting Christ into their hearts and for the baptismal service. The Nisei team conducted hymn singing and preaching services. And I had the privilege of baptizing the four new babes in the Lord. What a day of rejoicing it was!

A message has just come from the Tanii family that their four children want to be Christians and be baptized. I do not know how to express my joy in the Lord. In my heart I am shouting for this tremendous joy of seeing souls come to the Lord.

— Dateline: November, 1971

PHILIPPINES
LOVE CONQUERS FIERCE KILLERS
by General Missionary Board

THE Magahats, known as the "killers" of the Manobo tribe, are no longer enemies of the Philippine government. The final stage of reconciliation between this tribe, which lives in the mountains of Agusan Province, and the government was achieved when the Rev. Walter Groesbeck, superintendent of the Philippine Mission, recently introduced the leader, Datu Taglion, to the governor of Agusan.

Mr. Groesbeck first heard of the Magahats when he began mission work in the Philippines in 1949. Other Manobos told him they were killers and that it was too dangerous to try to reach them. He wanted to follow their trail up the mountain and preach to them but the field was large and the workers few, so he was unable to fulfill that desire during his first term.

When he and Mrs. Groesbeck returned to the field in 1955, the Lord gave them a Manobo convert, Rufino Delfinado. They had known Rufino when he was a high school student at Bunawan. He spoke the same dialect as the Magahats and as a boy of fifteen he had visited them during their heathen harvest festival. When Mr. Groesbeck began his first trip to the Magahats, Rufino went along as interpreter.

In July of last year Byrd Brunemeier, missionary for the New Tribes Mission, came to the Free Methodist missionary headquarters in Butuan City. He wanted to go into uncivilized areas in the mountains to get photographs of tribal people to interest young men and women in missionary work. Mr. Groesbeck helped him arrange a trip with a guide to the Magahats.

Byrd spent one night with them and came back with an encouraging story of the friendliness of the tribe and the desire of the men to hear the message from God. They talked to him about coming out of the mountains, but the leader was afraid government authorities would take him to prison. He requested a statement that no case was pending against him. Byrd told the leader he would ask Mr. Groesbeck to get a statement from the court and from the Philippine Constabulary to take back to him.

The burden that Mr. Groesbeck had felt in the past for these people now came back to him. He felt he could not hesitate. They wanted to know the true God. He must tell them.

The authorities willingly gave him the required papers. They were ready to forgive the deeds of the past if they could make the Magahats peaceful citizens.

For a guide he secured Mendoza, a Magahat who had come out to civilization several years ago and the same man that had gone with Byrd. Rufino consented to go as interpreter.

Mr. Groesbeck, Mendoza, and Rufino began the trip to the Magahats on the morning of August 13. It was a long and hazardous journey. Just as night was closing in they reached their destination. Two Magahats were waiting for them at the river. They told Mendoza that their leader, Datu Taglion, was a half-day hike away, and invited the three men to stay in their home.

In the afternoon of the second day Mr. Groesbeck met the leader. He was seated on the floor of his house and in a circle about him were ten men. After shaking hands Mr. Groesbeck told him how he had wanted to come seven years ago, and that he was sorry that he was so slow in coming.

The leader in turn told him about wanting to become a Christian, and how God had revealed to him years ago that an American would come and tell him about the true God. He added that in a dream the night before God had shown him that an American had come so he must hurry home.

After handing Taglion the documents and speaking to him about moving the families out of the mountains, Mr. Groesbeck talked of Jesus Christ and his power to overcome the evil spirits. Taglion and his men were interested and expressed their desire to be Christians.

When Mr. Groesbeck made a second trip to the Magahats in September, he took along his P.A. system and gospel recordings in Manobo. He held a service and let Taglion speak over the microphone.

He was on his third trip to the Magahats when he introduced the governor to Datu. The tribal leader came to the last barrio of Langasian to meet the governor and his party. At this meeting final arrangements were made for the Magahats to move out of the mountains and set up their barrio.

The government had tried to contact Datu Taglion for years to invite him to come out of the mountains, but he was always fearful and would not appear for a meeting. The love of a missionary drew him out. That same love made possible the reaching of his tribe with the gospel.

— Dateline: March, 1957

PHILIPPINES

Florencia's Uncle
by Naomi Thorsen

It began in a home in a remote mountain village in Upper Agusan in the Philippines. An elderly couple, Mr and Mrs. Sarapio Banez, sat at an engagement presentation.

Jose Havana had come to ask the hand of their niece, Florencia Gomez, in marriage. Mr. Banez, acting on the behalf of his dead brother, Florencia's father, was to lead the family in the decision — approval or rejection. Both the niece and her fiance were Christians. Mr Banez was not.

But his heart was not hard. It had been softened by acts of kindness and love on the part of Florencia. There was the time his daughter lay dying of tuberculosis and had to go to Butuan City for treatment. Florencia had lovingly led her to the Lord and cared for her many weeks until she could return to the mountains. Mr. Banez's heart had been moved by his daughter's radiant witness before her death.

Then more recently his only son, Romeo, had left the mountains to attend high school. His niece had once again opened her home in Butuan City. While there he, too, had opened his heart to Jesus.

And Jose Havana's life had surely been transformed. He was from the same mountain area, and Mr. Banez had known him well. Now he was in training in Light and Life Bible Seminary, to give his life to tell others about Jesus.

So it was with interest that Mr. Banez entered a conversation with one of the guests, a Free Methodist pastor from a nearby church. The pastor began to tell him once again about Jesus and His gift of eternal life. He responded with many questions. Finally his expression changed. For the first time he seemed to grasp the meaning and possibilities of faith. As he left the party, he could not get away from the things he had heard.

The seed was beginning to grow. It had been dropped in his heart a few years before but had seemed to lie dormant. Now — slowly and imperceptibly to the natural eye — it began to sprout.

A few weeks after the presentation ceremony Mr. Banez and his wife made the trip down from the mountains to Butuan City to visit their son and niece. On Sunday morning they attended a service in a church for the first time in their lives. They sat and listened intently and seriously. No one saw the seed open and begin to unfold.

As the Sunday school teacher made plain the eternal truths, and then as the pastor spoke, the Holy Spirit tenderly called Sarapio Banez to repentance. Because everything was new and strange, he sat still as the invitation was given at the close of the service.

But this new life budding in his heart gave him no rest. It required outward action. So as soon as he reached his niece's home, he told her he wanted to give his life to Christ.

As a "token" or external expression of his decision to turn from his sinful life, he wanted to burn his pipe and tobacco in the fire. His wife joined him and they knelt in prayer together as he gave his heart to God.

It was a sacred time; God was directing this altar service. As the fire consumed the instruments of a life-time habit that could lead to physical death, the gracious Holy Spirit removed the sin and guilt that could lead to eternal death. The result was as quick and effective in his heart as it was in the "token" fire.

By the time I arrived, the burning ceremony was over. I had missed it, but I did not miss the heavenly glow that shone on his face nor the transformation of spirit that God had just accomplished.

Immediately Mr. Banez began to share spiritual concepts that God was giving him. Not knowing how to read, he had not read the Bible. Yet he was sharing truths that are basics of a life in tune with God. For the next hour we sat and marveled how the Holy Spirit instructed him. It seemed that the recently sprouted seed had already come to full growth, and we rejoiced with thanksgiving to God.

"But," you ask, "what happened at the presentation?" You guessed correctly. Miss Florencia Gomez, former teacher in Light and Life Bible Seminary, is now married to the Rev. Jose Havana. Today they are working in those mountain villages, telling others of God's great love. The first year of their ministry they reported thirty-two adult conversions.

— Dateline: March, 1973

RHODESIA and MALAWI
TAMBO
by R. J. Jacobs

ONE of the first converts of the Lundi Mission in the district which lies south of the Nuanetsi River in Rhodesia was a lad, Simon, the eldest son of a drunken old heathen whose name was Tambo. For a long time Simon had to walk alone with God in that heathen kraal, but he was much concerned about the spiritual welfare of his parents and friends and often prayed for their salvation.

Tambo's village was built on a large granite rock close to our Maranda school and preaching center. Old Tambo was very friendly towards those who came to bring the gospel into the country of Chief Maranda, but his heart was dark and superstition ruled his life. He was dressed in true heathen style — a goat's skin hung from his loins, and on special occasions he produced an old, dirty shirt; the only civilized looking thing in his attire was a broad-brimmed, high-crowned hat which he himself had woven. One could almost imagine that one of the Pilgrim Fathers was approaching at first glimpse of the hat, before seeing what was walking underneath.

At times the missionary was accustomed to come to hold services or inspect the school, and his camp was usually made near Tambo's village. In the evening Tambo would usually come down from his rock to give his greetings, get the latest news, and to "bula" (gossip) with the white man. His wife, dressed only in a tanned hide hung about her waist, would come along behind, bringing with her the children. Then before they left, prayers would be announced, and there under the trees around the campfire a hymn would be sung, the Word read, and prayer made to God.

Who can tell how God got an audience in Tambo's old, sin-darkened heart? From the human viewpoint his case was hopeless, but with God all things are possible, and the Holy Spirit is still doing His work of convicting men just like Tambo of sin and righteousness and judgment. The first change that was noticed in his life was when he stopped going to the almost daily beer drinks in the neighborhood. When asked why he did not go, he replied that he was afraid of being poisoned by the other drinkers. Truly, the district was noted for its strong "medicine," and it was quite possible that his fears were justifiable. At any rate it was a step in the right direction, and the missionary encouraged him in the belief that home was the safest place for him. About this time an evangelist was sent to live near Tambo. He was a man of God who lost no opportunity to direct people to the Saviour. It was not long before the good word came that Tambo and his wife had repented and had believed in the Lord Jesus Christ.

In the office of the Lundi Mission there is a large battle-ax hanging on the wall. The long red handle is well decorated by many wrappings of colored wire. If it could speak, what a tale it could tell. It is old Tambo's battle-ax — not for killing human enemies but wielded many times in a vain effort to frighten away evil spirits, a weak and broken reed to fight demons. Tambo has exchanged this ax for the Sword of the Spirit. What a change salvation has made in this old heathen man! With a shining face he testifies that the desire for beer and tobacco has all been taken away. At the recent dedication of the Maranda church old Tambo, now clean and properly dressed, stood with many others to answer the questions asked of those entering the church on probation. In his hand instead of the battle-ax he clasped a brand new Tswa New Testament. He is unable to read a word, but he has learned to trust its Author.

A few months after his conversion, Tambo passed through his greatest test. While cutting grass for the new church roof he was bitten on the foot by a large puff adder. Shaking off the reptile, he cried for help, but it was some time before the people could get to him. In the meantime with terror gnawing at his heart, he tried to make his way to the evangelist's house, but the heat of midday and the exertion sent the poison quickly through his whole body. When the evangelist arrived, Tambo was on the ground near unto death. They carried him onto the rock near the new church, and then what was to be done? Fifty long miles to the Mission Station and Tambo even now half delirious. The evangelist sent a runner to the local trading store a few miles away in the hope that some snake-bite medicine could be obtained.

Afterwards, telling the story in his own simple way, the evangelist said, "As I knew nothing more to do, I just kneeled down beside old Tambo and prayed to God to save him." The answer to those simple prayers was not long delayed, and long before the boy returned from the store Tambo had passed the crisis. He was quiet and again in his right mind. A puff adder leaves a slow healing wound with sloughing of the surrounding flesh, but this was God's case, and a week later hardly any wound could be seen where the fangs entered.

The heathen say that the spirits of Tambo's ancestors were angry and tried to kill him because he became a Christian, but Tambo says it is God who made him alive from the dead.

— Dateline: September, 1945

RHODESIA and MALAWI
WARM DAYS AT LUNDI
by Beth Beckelhymer

SEPTEMBER, October, and November are summer months at Lundi Bible School. It is also the beginning of the rainy season; day by day the heat and humidity build up until it rains.

When the three small classrooms become unbearable, teachers and students pick up their books and search for a breezy place under a tree. Granite rocks in the schoolyard make good seats — for *short* classes.

During the winter term — May through August — we go outside to get warm. We have lights only at night, so when the classroom is dark and cold we look for a rock in the sunshine; and soon we are all warmed up and ready for study.

There are warm days of another kind at Lundi

— days that warm the heart. Graduation day, December 2, 1973, was such a day. The two graduating couples gave their testimonies.

It warmed my heart to hear Mrs. Phiri and Mrs. Ndlovu say confidently that they were going out with their husbands to serve the Lord. They had come to the school three years before as shy mothers, unable to read — and unsaved.

A few days before graduation it had also warmed the heart of their teacher, Elesinah Chauke, to watch them teach others to read — and then lead them to a knowledge of Christ — as they worked with outpatients at Lundi Clinic. God did much for both Mrs. Phiri and Mrs. Ndlovu during their three years at Lundi Bible School.

The last week of chapels had some warm days too. It was hot, muggy weather; but more important, our hearts were "strangely warmed" by the testimony of Moses Phiri. For three days he talked to us about what God had been showing him.

Moses was born in a Muslim family in Malawi, a small country northeast of Rhodesia. In school he studied the Scriptures, and this led to his conversion. While working as a bartender he had a dream of a man telling him to leave that work and become a pastor.

In Malawi, Moses couldn't get any training on his educational level, and God led him to Rhodesia and Lundi Bible School. Without money or relatives here, the Phiris often felt God's help in meeting their needs. As they gave love to others they found love and fellowship coming back to them and their two small sons, Eric and Peter.

Sometimes there were *cool* days too — when there was no meat for the pot and their own people and language seemed far away. (Sometimes their teacher experienced cool days too. As I looked at the students in the English section I often wondered how many would continue faithful and eventually serve our church. Moses was from another denomination and we had no mission work in Malawi. Some of the students seemed pulled this way and that by various influences. Sometimes I asked myself, "Is my work worth it?")

At the end of his three years of study Moses accepted a pastorate with his denomination and ministered to Malawians living in Salisbury, Rhodesia's capital city. It was a satisfying venture for him, giving immediate service and security.

But the night of November 8, 1973, Moses had a dream. In his dream he saw the same person who had spoken to him in Malawi and told him to become a pastor. This time he was told, "Moses, return to Malawi and begin a Free Methodist Church there."

Moses told the Lord that he couldn't do that, for he had already accepted the Salisbury job. And besides, there would be no support for him and his family in starting a new church in Malawi.

However, Moses was overwhelmed by God's call and awakened his wife.

"But Moses," she said, "if God says to go, we must go even if we suffer."

Moses agreed.

The next night God again spoke through a dream. This time Moses saw himself setting out many little pawpaw trees. They grew quickly and bore much fruit. Many people came to pick the fruit.

Moses understood the meaning. The next day he explained about the pawpaw trees to Phil Capp, the principal.

"How can I train leaders for all these churches that will soon start?" he asked Phil.

Later that week a third dream made it even more clear that he was to go home and begin Free Methodist churches there. By this time Moses was eager to do so.

But God had one more sign for him! Pastor Luke Klemo also dreamed and saw God's work in Malawi for Moses. This warmed Moses' heart anew. Now he was sure beyond all doubt.

As Moses explained all these things to us in chapel, "Did not our hearts burn within us?"

Within four days of their graduation the little Phiri family began the ten-day train ride that took them home — home to build a home and a church.

— Dateline: March, 1974

RHODESIA and MALAWI

WE SAW THE PAWPAW TREES
by Beth Beckelhymer

THE first week in September Gayle Hershberger, Gertrude Haight, Elesinah Chauke, and I returned from a week in Malawi. We visited Moses Phiri and his family in Damba Village and spoke at the new churches in the area.

What inexpressible joy to see the complete faithfulness of God! Everything He showed to Moses in the three dreams He gave him at Lundi Bible School a year ago is coming to pass. At

Moses' home we saw the small mud and thatch church which has been built. There are ninety-two believers at Damba Free Methodist Church — the first Free Methodist church in Malawi.

We had services in the village four nights, with about eighty people sitting on the sandy ground to sing songs with Gayle and her autoharp, to listen to our interpreted "sermons," and to see the filmstrips we showed via car battery power.

The people treated us royally. We enjoyed the excellent Malawi rice and the *chambo* fish from Lake Malawi. It was a thrill to watch Moses Phiri conduct a fine service Sunday morning, baptize infants, and receive six new members.

One day we took a very small handpulled ferry across Chia lagoon channel to a new grass and bamboo church in a Moslem village where there are now fifty-five believers! They were wonderful to us.

At night more than three hundred excited people crowded into the village and were almost beyond control. Moses wanted us to leave, for he felt we might be in danger. But the crowd was not rough — just boisterous and unable to get seated and be quiet.

About one-third of them sat and tried to listen as the film was shown and Gertrude and Moses shouted the message. Despite all the hindrances, many raised hands indicated a desire to know Jesus Christ. God is blessing at Chia Free Methodist Church.

We also met with some wonderful believers at Zomba, the former capital. Many came for the night service and walked home by moonlight.

The next morning Moses was awakened at 5:00 by a chief who came and said, "I heard Moses

Phiri was here. I live four miles away. I have a large village. I want a church for my people." That was our last day in Malawi and it touched our hearts to hear Moses praising the Lord for another opportunity to plant more pawpaw trees.

At Blantyre, the largest city of Malawi, 275 miles south of Damba Village, we met some of the nineteen fine young men whom Moses has gathered for a church there. They asked for forms and letters to enter Bible school at Lundi. Moses is in desperate need of helpers and God is calling laborers. Some young married men are willing to come even though it means giving up good jobs — others in spite of their poverty.

The church in Malawi is a men's movement with chiefs and other community leaders cooperating. It is a work of God. It is the work of a humble, obedient servant of that God.

— Dateline: March, 1975

RWANDA

SPARED FOR SERVICE
by Marti Ensign

UNLESS you are connected with the medical profession you perhaps cannot imagine the tension in the operating room that sunny morning. On the table lay Epayineto Rwamunyana, district superintendent at Kibogora and church head of all our Rwanda work. Many people had been praying for him. You might have been one of them, since requests for prayer had gone out over the U.S. as well as Burundi and Rwanda.

My memory worked overtime on the events leading up to this important moment. The day they brought him in to Kibuye, stretched out in the back of Orcutt's station wagon, we were in the middle of Alliance meetings with about fifty extra people on the station. This proved a blessing because the next morning several of the leading pastors, along with a few missionaries went up to his hospital room and, while others prayed in other places, Epayineto was anointed and prayed for.

I remembered how he improved until he was able to attend the pastor's prayer retreat at Burenza. As we saw the Holy Spirit poured out service after service and then heard Epayineto's inspired message the last Sunday morning we wondered if God would not spare him to our work in Central Africa.

But always there was that lingering doubt. If his illness was cancer it could be a temporary reprieve. Skilled surgeon, Merton Alexander, would operate December 20th along with Dr. Len.

The night before his surgery, I took my Kirundi Bible with a few choice verses marked and went to cheer up this wonderful pastor. I freely confess it was I who left cheered and blessed by that encounter. After thanking me for the verses and words, he read me a few! Then he gave this testimony.

"I am not at all afraid of tomorrow. If I should die, it doesn't really matter. It would be so wonderful to be in heaven with Jesus. Only the work in Rwanda worries me a little, but I know the Lord Jesus will take care of that because it is His. I can only thank the Lord for this time He has given me in Burundi. I had that pastors' retreat and the privilege of holding that revival at Mweya Bible School."

Now the critical moment had come. Dr. Alexander worked along with Dr. Rowland (from the Danish mission), Dr. Len, and two nurses. "What's your diagnosis?"

"Too early to tell."

This kind of questioning finally terminated by the doctor straightening up and saying, "Definitely just appendicitis. The appendix was ruptured and caused all this inflammation and adhesions."

"Yes' ashimwe," we reacted automatically in Kirundi. Jesus be praised! Our praise deepened and grew as we watched the quick and complete recovery. How grateful we were that Pastor Epayineto Rwamunyana was able to arrive home to stand by his beloved people in the present crises.

— Dateline: June, 1964

SOUTH AFRICA
PRACTICAL POINTS FROM PONDOLAND
by J. W. Haley

FROM time to time something happens in the work that is a surprise to us missionaries and we learn of our mistaken attitudes toward the national church. We regarded them as children and they showed themselves to be men; we thought they were too poor to do any big thing, and they were waiting to be given a chance; we pitied their poverty and did not have the heart to ask them to support their own work, and they were greatly desiring to do something more for their Lord and to show to themselves and their people that even Africans can do things.

One of our first grade teachers from Fair View, a godly man, accompanied us to our last quarterly meeting in Pondoland. He preached in the Spirit, and with that added dignity that comes to a naturally dignified people when they have accomplished something out of common. The Fair View church is entirely self-supporting and builds its own schools. This is a matter of great satisfaction to them and they are anxious to get their people on the other districts to do likewise.

The Pondo people are rather more backward in that the gospel found them later. We were on the question, "Are there any complaints?" An evangelist arose and in a manner very characteristic of a few years ago, began to "cry." They were overworked, there not being enough paid evangelists to carry on. He had asked for wire to fence the mission site "of the missionaries," and his garden would be eaten if he did not get it fenced. He had worked sawing trees to keep up the place till his sides ached. The grass roof of the house "of the missionaries" in which he lived needed new grass. This reminded another evangelist that the windows were falling out of the church "of the missionaries" at his place and he wanted them repaired.

As soon as there was a breathing space we took our courage in both hands to answer, as we felt that this was all the work of the local churches.

We told them to put names of lay workers on the plan for the circuit and they could not only carry on but open many new preaching places; that we did not plan to appoint more paid evangelists and probably, as fast as the present ones fell out, we would look to the national church to replace them. The local church could fence the mission sites as these all belonged to them and would not be carried off in the pockets of the missionaries. The school children could cut grass and they could thatch "their" house. An offering could be taken at the other place and new windows bought, and we told them of the financial difficulties the mission boards were in and also what Fair View had done.

Our visiting teacher could hardly wait for me to sit down till he was on his feet. He verified the financial difficulties of the boards, saying that the American Board had declined to send any more missionaries to an old mission station near Fair View and had also declined to send a missionary to teach the theological classes, saying one of the national ordained men could teach the others. He showed how they at Fair View were raising all their own money and said it was no use to cry, but urged them to take hold like men.

They surprised us, showing how far we were out of touch with them and their ambitions. One after another rose and said how sweet were these words and how thankful they were to hear them. They did not know that the work was theirs and that they would be allowed to do these things. They would willingly put laymen on the plan, and they did so immediately. They would open new points and take offerings to repair the churches. Then the first speaker rose and said that it had been said that it is of no use to cry, "but I see that it does help, for had we not cried we would not have received these nice words."

Then came the reports of the preachers, and one reported twenty heathen had chosen the Lord, another seven, and another four, until fifty-four were counted for the quarter. Hallelujah! One was in a very hard place where the people would not come to meeting. He sought them in their kraals and an evangelist of the Spirit Church followed him and spoke openly against him, telling the people not to listen to him as he was only a police for the white people. Three months ago he had one inquiry. He was in the thick of it and could not believe that the woman really wanted to join us, so asked her if she knew him and the church he represented, as most of the churches drink and snuff. She said, "Yes," she knew he was of the Greenville church. One of her people had believed there and she had made up her mind that when she became a Christian she would be of that church as they did not drink and snuff. He now reported that four had chosen the Lord. "Is anything too hard for the Lord?"

— Dateline: December, 1930

SOUTH AFRICA

AFRICAN PATRIARCH PASSES
by J. W. Haley

IN 1902, when I was first introduced to Africa and Africans, one of the first men I met was Mpolosa Mqadi, then mature, slim, straight, and in every move a gentleman. He had "turned from idols to serve the true and living God and to wait for His Son from heaven." Like Paul this was to be thenceforth his vocation. He had preached the Word from the beginning for the very joy of it without thought of remuneration. Inevitably his hearers would have spontaneously given to him, had there been a need, and so the methods taught by the Holy Spirit in the New Testament would have naturally come into action. But the missionary, not being very well taught in these ways and with the very best intentions, offered him a wage from foreign money. It amazed him to think that anyone would offer him money to tell of the great joy of deliverance he had, and he kindly but firmly declined to receive it.

Had this spirit been encouraged, there might have been a self-supporting Zulu church from the beginning. The missionary, thinking he must be paid, continued to urge him to accept money, till finally he agreed, and so the principle was established that all workers were to be supported by foreign money. It naturally followed that the extension of the African church would thereafter be in direct ratio to the amount of money the mission could provide. This was not Paul's method, nor what the Holy Spirit taught this man.

While I had plenty of the vivacity of youth and more than enough of spiritual pride, it was my duty to give a Bible lesson weekly to a class of workers which Mpolosa attended. On one occasion I asked my class if they had read their Bibles through. They answered in the negative, which gave my pride a welcome opportunity to vaunt itself. I had read it through. I have never fogotten to this day the gentle and masterly way in which Mpolosa pricked the bubble by the smile and simple question, "You have read it through; what does it say?"

When opportunity was given he endeavored to take the course prepared for ministers, but no longer young, his eyes gave out. When the Missionary Secretary visited Africa in 1924 and offered the Fair View church an ordained pastor if they would support him, he had to give place to a younger man who could meet the educational requirements but who was inexperienced as a pastor. He bore this demotion, so foreign to Zulu tradition, patiently, loyally working under the new pastor, who leaned on him heavily. But in love feast, his countenance beaming, I heard him say that had he not been wholly sanctified he would not have stood down and let this boy be preferred before him.

But Jesus said, "He that humbleth himself shall be exalted," and the time came when he was ordained deacon, and then, by special permission of the Commission on Missions, the first elder of the South African Conference. Thus the chagrin caused by his temporary demotion was removed from all our hearts. Others were ordained later, including his eldest son. These are all supported by the African Church and are its pillars.

My wife and I, being on a visit to South Africa for our health, and hearing of his failing health, went to see him. He received us warmly, brushed up the floor, and spread a mat. After a short visit and prayer we left him, and some days later called again. He said all was well with his soul. With difficulty he kneeled and in prayer made request that now in his weakness his courage might not fail him.

After prayer I felt I should lay hands on his head and commend him to God, which I did, and we left feeling that it had been a hallowed place. We called again. He was weaker. We suggested that perhaps we should not have prayer, as the effort might be too much for him. But he said prayer could never harm him; that was the thing he wanted. So we prayed, then bade him adieu, and as we left the mission for three weeks, that was the last farewell. But the mound is there in the graveyard, among his friends, where what is mortal of this, a faithful brother minister and servant of Christ, rests. He was first to be saved, first in the church these fifty years, first to be ordained elder, and the first elder to meet his Lord.

— Dateline: July, 1944

SOUTH AFRICA
ENCOUNTER WITH A LION
by Trygvar Brauteseth

IN the Transvaal African townships we have six church buildings from 30 to 80 miles apart. Two of these churches are pastored by full-time pastors.

At one place there has been seemingly endless trouble. Satan has been doing his utmost to hinder the work of God. For years the missionaries have been trying to bring peace to this place but no real "break-through" had been achieved.

On arrival there, Moses (fictitious name) the new pastor who had been appointed to this church, began to experience opposition and hardships. One of the local leaders was intensely jealous and did everything he could to make it hard for the pastor. When he circulated rumors that Moses would not stay there very long, for he was making a plan, the church members began to fear for the life of their pastor.

On one occasion the pastor and a friend visited this man's home. After they had read God's Word and prayed, they were given food as is the African custom. The friend refused to eat because he knew the food had been poisoned. But Moses only smiled and said: "The Lord has sent me here and I am assured that He will protect me as long as I place my trust securely in Him!" He ate the food and suffered no ill effects.

Many were the times when he was threatened,

but he would not be moved. He always insisted that he was there to serve God and not man. This difficult situation continued for many months and during this time much prayer was offered to God. We thank the overseas prayer partners too, who helped place this matter before the throne of grace.

Finally one morning, his wife, Ruth, (fictitious name) related a dream she had during the night. She had dreamed that Moses was walking down a road when suddenly a lion leaped at him and attacked him. There followed a dreadful tussle, but after a long fight he overcame the lion. Moses said he wondered why his wife had been crying in her sleep that night. However, after she related her dream he immediately realized that God was speaking and he understood that God had already answered prayer! The two of them started to praise Him and it was an inspiration to share in their thankfulness and praise.

The next Sunday Moses felt led to preach from the text: "If any man be in Christ, he is a new creature. . . ." At the close of the service, much to everyone's astonishment, who should come walking to the altar but the "lion" himself! There had been no altar call, but the Spirit of God was working in a wonderful way! The "lion" said he was very fearful that he would die in his sinful state and go straight to hell. He said that his life was filled with fear and sin and he wept for mercy at the mercy seat. Let us remember: "For we fight not against flesh and blood, but against persons without bodies — the evil beings of the unseen world, these mighty satanic beings and great evil princes of darkness who rule this world." (Ephesians 6:12, *Living Letters*)

— Dateline: February, 1967

TAIWAN
MIRACLE CHURCH
by Mary Taylor Previte

I looked in disbelief. "Polished terrazzo floors and altar rail? Electric lights?"

We had stepped from the dust of a tiny path of a Formosan mountain village, a path flanked by tiny houses and thatch dwellintg, into —

"Our miracle church, we call it," explained our missionary guide. "They polished the terrazzo floors by hand — because at that time there was no electricity here in Tsao Pu. The altar, and corner pillars on the altar, they polished smooth in the same way. Often they rubbed until their fingers bled."

Her glance moved up to the small light bulb above the pulpit. "Their church had to be the most beautiful building around; electric lights included. It's operated by battery." She smiled. "Every once in a while, when the battery gets low, the church buys two round-trip bus tickets down the mountain — one ticket for the battery and one for its escort — to have the battery recharged."

I was fascinated. "Seems to be a higher-class village than some we passed."

"That's today. Tsao Pu is almost a Christian village now — almost every home has at least one Christian. When the villagers stopped drinking, they could afford to improve their homes. But a few years ago it was another story. Not one Christian!

"We had several young Tsao Pu men come to

the Bible school for a week each month to attend classes to introduce them to the gospel. Then, home they'd go — to share with their neighbors what they'd learned in Bible School.

"My first visit to this village was on a cool October day when the danger of typhoons was over. We drove up the mountain in a friend's car. We would have gone earlier in the season, but we had been told that roads were slippery and dangerous — unsafe till the summer monsoons were over.

"The head man of the village, a Mr. Hsie, was the official representative from his area to the island's central government, and we were invited to sleep at his home. It was all very awkward: we couldn't speak a word of their language, nor they ours. A young fellow who had escorted us to the village interpreted, through Japanese, all our conversation. The Hsie family stood at a distance watching every move of these strange foreigners. Our eating fascinated them. We had brought crackers and cheese, and they provided hot water for us to drink."

"Was this your first trip to a mountain villge?" I interrupted.

"The first of many, many, many. While we're waiting, let me tell you the story of this remarkable church. You know they make quite elaborate preparations to welcome visitors like you from America."

I nodded. I could see she had told the story many times, obviously with no loss of enthusiasm.

"Our service the first night was held in the open space in front of the Hsie home. In that first service, it looked as though everyone from the three adjoining villages was there. We never knew how much they got from the message. It had to be translated for them from our Chinese, through Japanese, into their Paiwan language. But at least they could see the colored slides. I've always loved showing those slides of the crucifixion to people who have never seen them before, to help them understand the love of Christ for them through His death on the cross.

"Later, the Hsie family very graciously showed us our beds on their clean wood floor, where we spread our blankets and slept.

"On my next visit, the interpreter and I went alone. Again the Hsies entertained us in their home, but the service that night was in the home of one of the young men who had become a Christian.

"After the service, returning to the Hsie home, we found Mr. Hsie and his brother-in-law sitting across the table from each other, a now-almost-empty crock of homemade moonshine between them. As you can guess, neither of them had attended the evening service. A potent stuff, these mountain people make! Both men were under the influence of the liquor. What to do? Dare I spend the night in that home? Only a sliding Japanese paper door separated me from that drunken man!"

She paused. I could see by her faraway stare that she was more with her memory than she was with me.

"Do you remember the verse, 'He giveth his beloved sleep'? It's true, you know! Committing myself to God's care, I fell asleep right away.

"Different ones tried to talk to Mr. Hsie about the gospel. Nothing reached him. There was always the language barrier. We had no true Christian in their tribe who was able to couch our important religious terms in their language. They have no word for righteousness, no word for holiness. How could we make him understand?

"It was a Mrs. Wang whom God finally used. Her husband had formerly been the tribe's highest official. They were greatly loved and respected. Mrs. Wang, a Taiwanese church member, was in Tsao Pu transacting business, and she stopped at the Hsie home. As she tried to talk to Mr. Hsie about his soul, he suddenly burst out: 'I wish that someone who knows something about this religion would explain it to me. One comes and tells me it means this. Another tells me it means that. Another contradicts them both. So I have nothing to do with it.'

"God had sent the right messenger at the right time. Mrs. Wang carefully explained to him what it meant to repent and to be born again. She told him what it would mean to him. She invited him to give his heart to Jesus that very day. As they knelt, Mr. Hsie poured out his sins before God. Peace and assurance of sins forgiven came to him. He arose from his knees determined to throw all his energies into the local church, to buy a Japanese Bible from which he could learn more of the Christian religion, and to help lead his neighbors and friends to God.

"He went into immediate action. After a week or two of meeting in a home for services, Mr. Hsie commented to some of the young men: 'This plan of meeting is embarrassing. Here we meet in a home where only one member is a Christian. We want to have a service; the rest of the family wants to sleep. Embarrassing for us all. Let's have our own church — maybe bamboo, covered with thatch!'

"They built the church with their own hands. But it would hold only thirty people. In no time it was packed out.

"Do you know what they did? Now remember, this is a government official! Mr. Hsie again organized the mountain young people and Christians. This time, to build their church, they formed a line from the riverbed to the building site, passing stones from hand to hand through the human line. As the stones reached Mr. Hsie, he personally laid the foundation for the new church — one that would seat a hundred people. The new structure was built around the original tiny church.

"Every person in the congregation was a soulwinner. Mr. and Mrs. Hsie, highly esteemed in the community, kept inspiring the others to work for the Lord. Soon the congregation had outgrown the second building.

"Now Mr. Hsie urged his people to give all they could so they might build a third church — one that would seat the whole group at once. The people raised silkworms and denied themselves the necessities of life in order to get the foundation started. Again they formed the stone line from the riverbed. Again, Mr. Hsie stood at the end with his trowel and mortar, putting the stones into the big foundation. 'We will go as far as we can with the money the Lord helps us to give,' he said. First they laid a firm foundation around the other church. Then they had enough money to erect the walls.

"One of the chief sources of money, of course, was Mr. Hsie. He sold a piece of timberland for $10,000 and gave nine-tenths to the Lord for the church. His neighbors scoffed: 'A man with four children to educate away from home and who gives away nine-tenths to the church is crazy. Your children will lack, and their education will go unfinished.' But, as you can guess, the church was finished and the children have never once lacked money for tuition when it came due.

"Mr. Hsie inspired the people to make their church the most beautiful building around. You noticed the terrazzo floors a moment ago. Mr. Hsie also found orchids and exotic ferns on the hillside to place on the platform. The church was dedicated free from debt.

"Next Mr. Hsie urged the people to erect a parsonage. You see, he fully believed the time would come when the Lord would send them a resident pastor. It's a beautiful parsonage, and their latest project is the construction of a kindergarten to be used for Sunday school classes.

"Call a Sunday school convention at some central place — the largest delegation always comes from this church! At youth camp, look for the largest group to represent Tsao Pu. Theirs is a model Sunday school.

"Long ago, Mr. Hsie resigned from any official position. 'I served the devil for years,' he says, 'and now, in what time I have left, I want to give my best to the Lord.' He tills his land in the mountains to support himself and his family, but his main efforts are expended to promote the church. Unobtrusive, he never seems to be pushing people to do something; but by his own example, he inspires them in humility and stewardship. You can see why this is the second largest Free Methodist Church in Formosa.

"Model layman — model church."

— Dateline: November, 1966

ZAIRE

FROM SHOEMAKER TO TRANSLATOR
by Gerald Bates

From the northwest shores of Lake Tanganyika in the Congo, the Babembe people — farmers and fishermen with a keen sense of trade — spread into Burundi and even to Nairobi and Dar es Salaam. Although the Babembe have had missionaries for forty years, most missionary work has been conducted in the trade language of Swahili.

In 1926, a Moslem couple gave birth to a son whom they named Abekyamwale. Ten years later the family crossed the lake to Burundi, settling in Bujumbura, where Abekyamwale entered primary school and completed six years of schooling.

About this time the Moslem lad first heard the gospel. It left him troubled and anxious. His sins rose up before him one by one. He had stolen money from his mother — but how could he break her confidence in him by confessing such a thing? He had stolen government money. Surely he could never put that right! But God's love continued to reach down to him in his fear and misery. On December 30, 1944, he came to the Lord, claiming Jesus' blood to cleanse him from all sin.

His first act was to go to his mother and tell her that he had stolen her money, and confess his faith in Christ. She would neither listen to what he had to say nor touch the money when he tried to return it. Rebuffed, he retired to pray about it, and that night God spoke to his mother in a dream. "You must take that money — I have saved your son."

Restitution to the government was less difficult than he feared, and he settled down to live a Christian life.

The following year Abekyamwale married a Bembe girl. He continued to receive instruction in the Christian faith. In 1947, he was baptized and chose the name of Joel.

As a family man, Joel needed a regular income, so he sought a trade to learn. Someone suggested shoemaking and told him that he would find expert teachers in Uganda. Leaving his wife and three children in Bujumbura, he went to Uganda in 1952 to learn how to make shoes and hats. His only desire was to learn a trade and learn it well; but while there, he discovered something he had never thought of — the value of one's own language. He noticed how the Baganda would spend hours discussing their language, delighting in its rich vocabulary. For the first time he began to think of his own language as something precious.

About six months later Joel returned to his home and set up shop. Several years passed, and business prospered. He expected to continue shoemaking for the rest of his days; but in 1956, God began speaking to him. When he went to church and joined in worship he envied the local people their good fortune in having hymns in their own language. Not one hymn existed in Bembe! He seemed to hear God saying, "Leave your shoemaking and translate hymns for your own people so they can sing my praises with understanding." Leave shoemaking? How could he support his family? Surely God could never mean this! But God's voice continued to speak, and he knew he would have no peace till he obeyed.

Other difficulties rose in his mind. Kibembe has glottal stops where the throat must constrict before pronouncing vowels and certain consonants. How could he write such sounds? At length he went to a missionary working among the Barundi and told her of his desire to translate hymns into his own language and of the problem he faced in writing the sounds. She wrote to an expert on Congo languages, who sent notes he had taken in a visit to Bubembe, and the problem was solved.

Now began a period of tremendous physical strain for Joel. During the day he continued his shoemaking as usual, but from 8 P.M. to 2 A.M. he shut himself up with a lamp and his books and worked on the hymns.

As each hymn was finished he submitted it to four close friends for criticism and help — a tailor, an orderly in the hospital, and two fishermen. They sang the hymns together, delighted at being able to sing in their own language, discussed the words, suggested improvements, and gave general encouragement.

Joel's long hours of work by feeble light took their toll and he found his eyesight failing. He prayed; the Lord sent him a gift of money, and he was able to buy glasses.

The following year Joel realized that God was waiting for him to rely on Him for everything, so he devoted himself entirely to the hymnbook, trusting the Lord for bodily needs. From here and there money came in, so that he and the family never went hungry.

This year, Joel had fifty hymns translated out of his goal of 300. Again he sought out the missionary who had helped him and asked how, if he ever got his hymns finished, he could have them printed. The printer from one of the missions was there. He assured Joel that when the book was ready, funds would be raised to print it.

At last the translation of the hymns was finished. The next task was to prepare them for press. How could they be typed? Again he prayed — and others with him — and a missionary gave him an old typewriter and showed him how to use it. Eventually the laborious task of typing was finished.

Now Joel sent messages to Bubembe country and asked representatives from the area's congregations to meet. On an agreed day, he and the others from his little "team" went over and sang the hymns, teaching them some of the words. "When can we buy these for ourselves?" "How soon can we have these hymns to sing in our services?" The questions were endless as the delighted people examined Joel's manuscript.

Joel had gone to Bubembe with a business proposition. "How many of you will buy these hymnbooks when they are printed? We can't tell yet how much they will cost, but it certainly won't be less than forty francs." A forest of hands waved in the air. "I will." "I will." Joel explained, "To print these books will cost money. Will you pay forty francs *now,* and your name will be written down; then, when the books arrive, all you will have to pay will be the remainder, if it costs more. In this way we can use your money to buy paper to print the books on." The people responded and enough money was raised to make the printing possible. In 1961, the manuscript went to press.

Independence came to Congo and the fighting which broke out disrupted mail and other services. It was not until the end of March, 1964, that 5,000 books were ready. Joel and some friends took these across the lake to Bubembe for Easter Day. What a happy Easter that was, as those who had paid their advance money came to bring the balance, and others pressed in to buy their copies.

After sending the hymns to press in 1961, the longing to have Scriptures in Bembe turned Joel to Mark's Gospel. A missionary had made an attempt at translating this in 1932, but the edition had long been out of print. Joel laid the matter before his four Bembe friends and they encouraged him, promising prayer support and all the help they could give.

Bembe has many dialects. It is difficult to express in a way which is acceptable to people from all parts of the country. So Joel traveled around Bubembe gathering information about the forms of speech most commonly used. In 1962, with the help of his four faithful friends, he finished the first draft of his translation of Mark.

Joel asked the Bubembe church to appoint a committee to check his translation of Mark. This committee, composed of two men from each of the five main dialect areas of the country, met in 1963 and worked on it, gradually achieving a translation acceptable to all. Joel is still correcting blemishes and listing points of uncertainty. He wants to call the committee together again before sending the manuscript to the British and Foreign Bible Society for publication.

When given the story of William Carey, Joel was delighted to find that this famous Bible translator had been a shoemaker like himself. He felt encouraged to persevere with the task God had called him to do. "The greatest desire I have in my heart," he says, "is that we may have the Scriptures in our own language before I die."

— Dateline: May, 1966

ZAIRE

THE FIVE-MILE LADDER
by Gerald Bates

I suppose from time to time people wonder if the modern, mechanized, mobile, gadget-laden missionary ever descends from his four-wheel drive safari wagon to walk on Africa's red dirt and trek into the outback like his hardier predecessors used to do.

This year the Zaire Conference deliberately set its annual pastors' retreat 25 kilometers back in the hills, far from any motor road, in order to show concern for some of the backcountry. With Mulele rebels roaming around up there not so long ago, this is probably the first year it would have been safe.

The discussion before retreat turned around to yours truly when, with some smiles, some of my African brothers asked me if I would be able to make it to the retreat this year! I could see they would kindly accept any reasonable excuse I could come up with — fully knowing it was 90 percent sure to be a cop-out, but also not wanting an ambulance case somewhere back in the bush.

Outwardly smiling as well — and inwardly vowing this Ohio farmboy would show them something about walking — I assured them confidently: "No problem, I'll be there!"

The months rolled by swiftly and I found myself approaching this commitment rather rapidly. I waited in vain for a face-saving malaria attack, but as the day neared I seemed to be in perfect health — no escape anywhere in sight!

So on the appointed day I started off down the lakeshore road in the Land Rover toward the take-off point for the interior. Along the way I picked up a couple of Zaire pastors and a refugee pastor from Burundi. Our conference youth director awaited us at the rendezvous point.

After a short night in the local teacher's house we rolled out at dawn — a quick cold water wash and a few bananas — and our procession filed up the trail through the morning mists. Startled eyes peeked out of doorways as we swung by, making good time before the sun got hot. Up ahead, rising into the sky, was the range of mountains that gives title to this story — the five-mile ladder.

The Zairians are a very direct, uncircuitous people and their trails reflect this basic trait. Where other tribes I know would have resorted to switchbacks, our trail tackled the mountain head-on, right up the face.

For five hours we toiled — clothes sweat-soaked as the sun came up, lungs stretching painfully as the altitude made itself felt. Some older members dropped behind. The rest of us — the Ohio farmboy still in there — climbed stubbornly on, one heavy foot in front of, *and 18 inches above,* the other.

Toward eleven o'clock, the sun hot on our

backs now, we reached the plain and began the more gentle rises and descents of the plateau region. No people — here and there some scrub bananas marking an old village site — but just a path leading on. Is there a village somewhere at the end, one wonders? The path itself is interesting — a trough, really, with wood fibers rubbed off on stones here and there. The men bring the dugout canoes down this path, dragging them by long ropes the whole twenty miles to the lakeshore.

As we go on we cross chilly mountain streams and pass through copses of huge straight trees — some of them 180 feet tall, seven feet through at the base. Some of the straight slender ones will make three dugout canoes end on end. We are stopped by a great pile of chips in the path; here is a dugout canoe still attached to the mother tree, the artisans off somewhere to their village.

After eight and one-half hours of hiking, with all the spring gone out of the leg muscles, we come to Kilumbi, host village for the pastors' retreat. Someone spots our column, drums strike up a lively rhythm, people boil out of houses laughing, singing, dancing. Men, women, and children surround our dusty company. We make a triumphal parade through the village until someone steers us toward the cool darkness of a grass-roofed house. One pastor stretches out and is instantly asleep leaving the burden of conversation to the waking world. Shortly we are called to a small room where there is a twenty-gallon pan of hot water. Twenty minutes later we emerge a new person — or almost, that is.

The weekend contained some of the most meaningful experiences we can remember. Our services were held in a round chapel, the floor covered with reed mats. Approaching it you would have been struck first — as I was — by the pile of shoes and sandals at the door, to keep the floor clean for sitting. Inside we had some wonderful services. I gave two meditation-Bible studies on I Peter 1. One evening we had a question-and-answer period and planning session on the future direction of our work.

One special prayer service was dedicated solely to prayer for more missionaries. One grizzled veteran from deep in the hills prayed one of the most touching prayers I have ever heard. It went something like this:

> **Now Lord, I want to send this prayer directly to America.**
> **To those who are in deep sleep, speak to them in a dream.**
> **For those who are traveling in their nice cars, ask them where they are going so fast.**
> **Speak to those on planes or in ships.**
> **Lord, you know we need help.**
> **Look at Lulenge! (one of our areas)**
> **Look at Burega! (another new work)**
> **Look at all our work.**
> **We need workers! We need missionaries!"**

I had an uneasy feeling that we were going over the General Missionary Board's head in this matter, but. . . .

Perhaps the best part of all was simple Christian fellowship, sharing together. One evening I had an impromptu prayer service with the local chief, a Christian with over 8,000 people in his area. He wanted prayer for strength and wisdom to withstand the temptations of political life.

In the quiet evenings we could look out over vast valleys toward Itombwe — still another mountain range further on, concealing more of our churches and schools. What an awesome vast terrain we have back in those hills, what needs, what opportunities, what rewards!

Our weekend concluded with a joyous Sunday-morning service, with introductions of about fifty pastors, superintendents, and school directors, and many seekers in response to the invitation. Monday morning we started out at 4:00 A.M. with kerosene lanterns. Coming down, it only took six hours. What a weekend! Yes, it was worth it — even the five-mile ladder.

— Dateline: January, 1973